GO BIG

The Marketing "Secrets" of Richard A. Viguerie

GO BIG

The Marketing "Secrets" of Richard A. Viguerie

**How Conservatives Can Win with Bigger and
MORE: Organizations, Donors, Money**

Richard A. Viguerie

American Target Advertising™, Inc.
Manassas

Words to Act On and Live By

"But this *I say*, He which soweth sparingly shall reap also sparingly; and he which soweth bountifully shall reap also bountifully." —2 Corinthians 9:6 (KJV)

"Much will be required from everyone to whom much has been given. But even more will be demanded from the one to whom much has been entrusted." —Luke 12:48 (ISV)

"There's no accounting for the amount of good a man can accomplish, if he makes a business of it." —Benjamin Franklin

In 2014, Professor Harry Jaffa of Claremont Institute said:

"Western Civilization survives because of America. America survives because of the Conservative Movement."

Richard A. Viguerie added:

"The Conservative Movement survives because of several hundred conservative leaders, spokesmen, donors, and activists. And without them, Western Civilization disappears."

About Richard Viguerie

"Dr. Lee Edwards [Senior Fellow, Heritage Foundation] has named Richard A. Viguerie one of 13 'Conservatives of the Century.' He noted, 'The Texas-born Mr. Viguerie became the king of political direct mail and provided conservatives with an essential tool to raise money, communicate ideas, and motivate people.'"

— *The Washington Times*
December 1999

"He is the catalyst who allowed conservatism to reach the pinnacles that it has over these past many years."

—Barry Goldwater Jr.

"The truth is I couldn't have gotten my institute off the ground without what I learned from him. Without any doubt, Richard Viguerie is the 'Funding Father' of the conservative movement. When he fights in the public policy process, his weight is always felt."

—Morton Blackwell
President, Leadership Institute

"He is one of the genuine pioneers of modern American politics. He went out and figured out some very complicated things and then applied them to a cause he believed in—a cause that I am proud to have worked with him on. The fact is, he really invented the use of direct mail by Republicans and conservatives."

—Newt Gingrich
Former House Speaker

"When interviewing potential campaign managers or general consultants, the first question you should ask is, 'What do you know about Richard Viguerie?' If they've never heard of him, you can end the interview right then and there."

—Chuck Muth
National conservative campaign consultant

"He has left his print on every aspect of the conservative movement, from its infancy to today."

—David Keene
Former President, National Rifle Association
Former Chairman, American Conservative Union/CPAC

"Richard Viguerie is probably the greatest political copywriter in American history. If you understand copywriting, you understand political communication. He really is the godfather of the conservative movement."

—Roger Stone
New York Times
Bestselling Author, Political Consultant

"Richard Viguerie is simply the best! He and his talented staff enabled us to set fundraising records that helped carry us to victory in November."

—Hon. Ken Cuccinelli
Former Attorney General of Virginia

He is "one of the creators of the modern conservative movement."

—Alexander Cockburn
The Nation
February 14, 2008

"Before Rush Limbaugh, there was Richard Viguerie. But before Rush, conservatives for nearly 40 years looked to Richard Viguerie, the founding father of the conservative movement, for the 'right word' on policy and politics. Before Mr. Limbaugh, it was Mr. Viguerie whose mail was delivered over hill and dale, through rain, sleet and snow, to conservative donors and activists, prodding them to take action. Legions of candidates, from the courthouse to the White House, have benefitted from Mr. Viguerie's expertise, and legions of others have tasted defeat as a direct result of his ability to raise money and promote action simply by sitting down at his typewriter."

—Jim Martin
The Washington Times

"We talk a lot about changing your life with copywriting. But Richard Viguerie did more than just change his life: He changed the world. Richard Viguerie is one of the most brilliant copywriters who ever lived, a truly iconic figure in the history of direct marketing, and a living testament to the power of copywriting to make a difference in the world."

—Richard Armstrong
Author, *The Next Hurrah:*
The Communications Revolution in American Politics

John F. Kennedy Jr's magazine, *George,* listed Viguerie's pioneering of political/ideological direct mail in the 1960s and 1970s, which enabled grassroots Americans to participate in the political process to a greater degree than ever before, as one of the "defining political moments of the 20th century."

—*George Magazine*

"The Richard A. Viguerie Company aided Reagan's electoral sweep and the Republicans to gain control of the Senate. . . ."

—*U.S. News and World Report* (1981)

"Richard Viguerie, the direct mail impresario . . . may have understood the value of a name before anyone else in contemporary politics."

—*New York Times Magazine*

He is "the architect of the New Right."

—*The Baltimore Sun*

"The father of political [direct marketing]."

—*Direct Magazine*

"When you lose an election, you think, 'If only Ronald Reagan wasn't on the ballot,' or 'If only he hadn't had Richard Viguerie and his mass-mailing operation out in Falls Church, I would have won.'"

—Congressman Jerry Patterson (D–VA)

The new-fashioned conservatives' use of direct mail "may have tipped the entire political balance" in their direction, and "to a remarkable degree, the story of that development is the story of one man: Richard A. Viguerie."

—David Broder, *Washington Post* political reporter and nationally syndicated columnist (1980)

"In the rapidly evolving and growing nether world of conservative politics, a 'new right' is emerging and Richard A. Viguerie is its godfather. Both his friends and enemies acknowledge that if Richard Viguerie succeeds in fulfilling his dream, American politics may never be the same."

—John Fialka
The Washington Star
June 23, 1975

Dedication

There are numerous people to whom I considered dedicating this book. Over the 60 years I've been involved at the national level of the conservative movement, I've been blessed to know most of our best and most important leaders.

As you read *GO BIG*, you'll see the importance I place on the need for principled conservative leaders with high energy and bold, aggressive, entrepreneurial spirits who have strong moral beliefs, values, and character. Fortunately, this description of successful national conservative leaders fits a number of conservatives.

The primary purpose of writing this book is to encourage hundreds of thousands of conservatives (mostly young) to launch and/or become active in conservative organizations by devoting a significant amount of their time, energy, talent, and treasure to protecting, preserving, and passing on to future generations the blessings of freedom and liberty.

However, there is only one conservative who fits the above description perfectly and has also

- trained 250,000 conservatives via 54 different training schools; workshops, and seminars to be effective in the public policy arena;
- been a role model to thousands of conservatives of all ages;
- launched or helped launch many important conservative organizations;
- helped elect more conservatives to public office than anyone; and
- helped elect to a political party office more conservatives than anyone.

I've just described my dear friend, the founder and president of the Leadership Institute, Morton C. Blackwell, to whom I am pleased to dedicate this book.

In the spring of 1973, Dr. Lee Edwards invited me to join him and a 32-year-old young conservative, Morton Blackwell, for lunch at the Mayflower Hotel. Lee and his wife, Anne, have been dear friends to me and my wife, Elaine, since the early 1960s. However, I had never met or heard of Morton, even though in 1964 he was Senator Barry Goldwater's youngest elected delegate at the Republican National Convention in the Cow Palace, San Francisco, California, as well as a national leader in the College Young Republicans.

The meeting went so well that I invited Morton to have lunch with me 10 days later, again at the Mayflower.

At the end of the second lunch, Morton said, I spoke magic words to him. They were, "Morton, I'd like for you to come work with me and help me build the conservative movement."

Morton said later that he would have taken a pay cut to have the job. He was making about $14,000 a year at the American Enterprise Institute, and my offer included a very modest pay increase.

Morton indeed came and worked with me and our team at The Viguerie Company. His informal title at our company was Ambassador without Portfolio to the Conservative Movement. Morton represented me at hundreds of conservative meetings in the Washington, D.C., area and around the country. We started a bi-weekly newsletter reporting on the growing conservative movement with Morton as the editor—*The Right Report*.

Morton left in 1979 to work on the staff of newly elected New Hampshire U.S. Senator Gordon Humphrey. Morton's next professional move was in 1981, when he became a special assistant to President Ronald Reagan.

All of this helped make Morton an important conservative leader. However, Morton's most important work was ahead of him when he launched the Leadership Institute (LI) in 1979, a 501(c)(3) nonprofit educational foundation, with 62 donors the first year. LI's mission is to increase the number and effectiveness of conservative activists and leaders in the public policy process.

In 2021, Morton's Leadership Institute had more than 92,000 active donors and a total revenue of more than $30 million. Today, the Leadership Institute has 113 employees who conduct 54 different types of training schools, including Student Publications Workshop, Broadcast Journalism School, Campaign Management School, Youth Leadership School, Future Candidate School, and Public Speaking Workshop–Advanced.

Some 649 different training sessions were conducted in 2021 alone. Since 1979, the Leadership Institute has conducted more than 7,000 training schools attended by more than 250,000 graduates (mostly in their twenties), learning how to be effective in the public policy arena. The 250,000 includes my son, Ryan; granddaughter, Ginny; governors; senators; congressmen; and state legislators. This does not include mayors, city council members, and other GOP political leaders too numerous to count.

In a 2021 creative meeting with our company's client, Hillsdale College, someone asked the 20 people in the room to mention the name of an organization that they would select to contribute to if they could only contribute to one organization—and it couldn't be Hillsdale or their church. When it was my turn, I said "Morton Blackwell's Leadership Institute because I don't know the name of any other conservative organization that has had more impact on America than LI."

Can you think of anyone who's trained 250,000 conservatives to be active and effective in political campaigns, the government, public policy organizations, and the private sector?

As Ronald Reagan said about America's future, "You ain't seen nothing yet." I feel the same way about Morton Blackwell and his Leadership Institute.

In the last four or five years, LI has been growing at about 25% per year. A few years ago, after a meeting at the Heritage Foundation, I gave Morton a ride to his office in Arlington, Virginia. During the ride, I asked him how his most recent year was. I've asked this question of many leaders of conservative organizations, and invariably they will start the conversation by talking about how many new donors they got or how much money they raised.

However, Morton didn't mention donors or income, he talked about how many people he had trained, how many conferences LI had conducted, and the effectiveness of the people that had been trained in the past year.

In 2017, the Leadership Institute also began to conduct annual international training for foreign conservative, free-market, anti-communist leaders.

No description of Morton's contributions to the conservative cause would be complete without including his late wife of 47 years, Helen. Morton and Helen were a perfectly matched and yoked team. Helen shared all the important personal attributes I recognized in Morton, except hers were wrapped in a beautiful, petite, feminine woman.

For decades, literally thousands and thousands of young conservatives ate and slept at Helen and Morton's Arlington, Virginia, home. Many a future governor, senator, and congressman had dinner and hours of political-movement-building conversation there, then slept in the guest bedroom, on the basement sofa, or on the floor in a sleeping bag.

Helen served as Virginia state chairman of Phyllis Schlafly's Eagle Forum for 25 years, writing a regular national syndicated column, and held many other important positions in national, state, and local organizations, including serving on the Board of Visitors for James Madison University.

After hosting thousands of young conservatives over decades, Helen wrote a delightful pamphlet, *Crash Course in Courtesy* (see Appendix 4). It is a "How To" book for young people on how to be a good guest. A copy can be acquired at www.leadershipinstitute.org. Unfortunately, Helen passed away far too soon, in September 2019.

By the way, I've known Morton and Helen's son, William, almost since the day he was born. He is the same age as my son, Ryan. Years ago, I saw William in our office and said, "William, what are you doing here?" He said, "I work here." So, William got a job at American Target Advertising without anyone knowing who he was, which pleased him and his parents greatly. Twenty years later, William continues to be a valued part of our company's team.

Morton Blackwell and Richard Viguerie at a Conservative Foundation
Reception, May 2022, in Washington, D.C.

Contents

Words to Act On and Live By. . . . . *v*
About Richard Viguerie. . . . . *vii*
Dedication. . . . .*xi*

1: How It All Began 7
2: Viguerie's Four Horsemen of Marketing® 13
3: Brand Yourself, Brand Your Organization—
    Change Your Life, Change the World. 16
4: Do You Have a Tagline? 20
5: Brand Democrats and Govern America. 24
6: Newt's Four-Part Plan 33
7: Needed: 20,000 New Single-Issue Conservative
    Organizations 38
8: How and Why to Acquire New Donors 46
9: A Scary Look at Liberal Dark Money and Grassroots
    Marketing. 52
10: Now, Here's Some Good News 56
11: Nationalize the 2022 and 2024 Elections 61
12: "It's the Primaries, Stupid" 66
13: The State of the Conservative Movement and What's
    Needed to Win and Govern America. 75
14: Internet Marketing 81
15: Viguerie's DOs and DON'Ts of Marketing 85
16: What You Can Do to Save America 92
17: Some Firsthand Stories of How Conservatives Used Direct
    Mail to Build the Conservative Movement—And Win. . .100
18: Are You Being a Good Steward of Your Nonprofit's
    Money? 117
19: 11 Big Mistakes Conservative Leaders Make 122

20: Going Big Safely within the Law (by Mark Fitzgibbons). .132
21: How to Grow 10×=1,000% (by Kathleen Patten) 139
22: American Target Advertising's Past, Present, and
     Future Role in the Conservative Movement 145
23: A Call to Arms 151

Acknowledgments 160

Appendix 1: Richard A. Viguerie's Direct Marketing/
     Fundraising Suggested Reading List 162
Appendix 2: Conservative Organizations, News, and
     Learning. 163
Appendix 3: The Laws of the Public Policy Process. 170
Appendix 4: Useful Guides 173
Appendix 5: 100 Largest Right-of-Center Nonprofits 174
Appendix 6: 100 Largest Left-of-Center/Progressive
     Nonprofits 179
Appendix 7: 20 Largest Private Conservative Family
     Foundations 183
Appendix 8: 20 Largest Private Liberal Family Foundations .184
Appendix 9: Photographs 186
Appendix 10: Podcasts and Videos 190
Appendix 11: Books by Richard A. Viguerie 191
Appendix 12: Viguerieisms 192

Index 195

Survey for *GO BIG* Readers. 202

Introduction

In 1776, America's Founders lit the light of liberty that is now in danger of being snuffed out by the actions of Democrats, the weakness of Republican politicians, and inactions of conservative leaders.

Whether the Democrats call themselves liberals, progressives, or socialists, they are fast moving America towards the darkness of Marxism/communism.

Sound unrealistic? It's been said many times by communists that "the goal of socialism is communism."

So why are most national, state, and local conservative leaders AWOL in the Spiritual Civil War raging in America? The Democrats have so much energy, at times it seems you can almost cut it with a knife—not so with most conservative leaders.

The motto of the Catholic charity The Christophers is, "Don't Curse the Darkness, Light a Candle." In recent decades, conservatives have been good at cursing the darkness of the Democrats' ideas, policies, and programs but have failed at effectively opposing them.

My friend Kevin Gentry, vice president of Stand Together, said to me, "The lack of experimentation and risk-taking is maddening. Have our folks lost the will to win?"

One afternoon a few years ago, I was ranting to Kathleen Patten, president and CEO of our company American Target Advertising, about how badly conservatives are losing, and how the Left is not only winning but is gaining ground and leaving us behind. Kathleen said to me, "Most conservative leaders have low energy."

Wow, I thought, that's it—most conservative leaders lack the energy of the Left.

In 2019, I was in a meeting with about 18 national conservative leaders, and I made this exact point about "lack of energy by conservative leaders." The president of one of our very best organizations joined in and agreed with me. He said that he had only been able to identify about 12 national conservatives who had high energy. Later, I did my own list, and I could only get up to about nine or 10, not 12.

Those who oppose liberty (Democrats) are winning, not by the superiority or success of their ideas, policies, or programs, but by the weakness of Republican politicians and the inactions of conservative leaders.

America is about half Democrat and half Republican, so how can we be losing so badly to ideas, policies, and programs that have always failed? Why is half of America voting for socialist/Marxist candidates? Is socialism/communism more appealing than liberty/freedom?

There are a number of reasons, one of which is that the Left, for over 100 years, has had a plan and an agenda, and conservatives have not.

There's an old saying that the person with a plan, an agenda, and limited resources will accomplish far more than the person with greater resources who has no plan, no agenda, and acts intermittently.

Since the early 1900s, the Left has had a plan, and they are working their plan. They won the cultural war years ago— today the hard Left controls all of the commanding heights. The leadership of every major institution in America is arrayed against conservatives, including Big Media, Big Tech, Hollywood, entertainment, national radio and TV, the non-profit community, the legal community, higher education, lower education, Big Business, Wall Street, unions, organized religion, and of course the massive bureaucracy of government, including the Justice Department, IRS, the military, the FBI, and the CIA.

Because there are a number of reasons we are losing—and I can't cover them all in this book—due to my expertise in marketing, I'm going to focus on marketing as one of the major reasons and explain how we can reverse the move of America towards Marxism and move America back to the ideas brilliantly stated by Thomas Jefferson in the Declaration of Independence.

About every six weeks I write a marketing memo that I send to ten thousand conservative leaders, marketers, activists, and major donors, with advice, suggestions, and recommendations about how to grow conservative organizations, launch new ones, raise more money, acquire more supporters, BRAND themselves and Democrats, become more effective, and govern America.

After four years of writing the memos, I've seen very little growth in the conservative movement, but I see a lot of continuing growth and energy on the Left. So, I decided to put my ideas, suggestions, advice, and recommendations into a book that will be available to all conservatives.

Hopefully, many good things will happen as a result of this book, including . . .

- conservatives (mostly under age 40) will launch 20,000 new single-issue nonprofits,
- hundreds of thousands of conservatives will volunteer to help these new organizations with leadership and significant financial support and/or help in whatever way they can,
- leaders of existing conservative organizations will be encouraged to significantly grow their nonprofits—some by 100%, others by 1,000%,
- members of boards of directors of conservative nonprofits and major donors will pressure their organization's leadership to sow bountifully in order

to reap bountifully, and if not, to replace them with high-energy, effective leadership,

- many conservative leaders and candidates for public office will learn how to market their organizations and themselves better, build a large team of supporters, raise lots of money, BRAND themselves and the Democrats, and win.

Soon after I launched the world's first ideological/political direct mail/direct marketing agency in January 1965, conservatives quickly and quietly began to dominate grassroots marketing. That continued through most of the 1980s, not only through my agency but also as some of our executives went out to start new organizations or their own agencies.

Throughout the 1960s and 1970s, most of the Left ignored grassroots marketing and relied on unions, foundations, and the government (taxpayers) as their primary source of money. However, today the Left dominates grassroots marketing, so much so that conservatives are not competitive.

In the last eight presidential election cycles (1992–2020) the GOP received less than 50% of the popular vote in every election, except one (2004).

Since Trump's presidency in 2017, the Left annually raises about 700% more money than conservatives ($21+ billion vs. $3–4 billion) for their ideological organizations from about 700% more donors (21+ million vs. 3–4 million).

Consider these examples:

The Democrats Have Left Conservatives Far Behind in Grassroots Marketing

- From July 2016 to June 2017, Planned Parenthood added 1.3 million new donors to their file (*Planned Parenthood 2016–2017 Annual Report,* p. 17). Know any pro-life organizations with even 100,000 new donors in the last 12 months? Me neither.

- The ACLU raised $93 million online in the first 12 months after Trump was elected president vs. $5.5 million the 12 months before (*Politico,* "ACLU to Storm 2018 Midterms," Jan. 6, 2018).
- ActBlue, in the 2019–20 presidential election cycle, had 13.4 million people who gave them their credit card information to make quick and easy donations to liberal candidates and causes. ActBlue, in the 2019–20 presidential election cycle, raised $4,318,377,981 (that's billions) (Actblue.com, "Billions raised online since 2004"; OpenSecrets.com, "ActBlue 2019-2020 Cycle).
- In 2019, all Democrats running for the Virginia House of Delegates and the State Senate had 274,000 donations of $200 or less—all Republicans had 19,000. Any wonder why the GOP lost the Virginia House of Delegates and the State Senate in that election (Virginia Public Access Project)?
- I estimate the Left has about 20,000 single-issue nonprofits, and conservatives have about 1,000–2,000 (Progressive-sites.net; SourceWatch.com; Wiki list of Progressive Organizations/Conservative Organizations). Every nonprofit needs a president, vice president, secretary/treasurer, fundraiser, director of membership, media, events, etc., which provides the 20,000 liberal organizations with a massive leadership pool. From this pool of 100,000+ activists/leaders come future Democrat candidates for city council, mayor, state legislature, Congress, etc. Remember, Barack Obama's job description before running for the U.S. Senate in 2004 was "Community Organizer."

At age 89 (born September 23, 1933), I still work/focus 12–13 hours a day, five and a half days a week (never on Sunday). I don't personally know anyone at any age who keeps up with me.

I've been blessed with good health and enjoy what I do. I'm at the top of my game—I've never been better—I'm a better marketer today than at age 80 and significantly better than when I was 70.

I try to follow, and I urge you to do the same, Jesus's instructions: *"When someone has been given much, much will be required in return; and when someone has been entrusted with much, even more will be required"* —Luke 12:48 (NLT), and

"He who sows sparingly will also reap sparingly, and he who sows bountifully will also reap bountifully" —2 Corinthians 9:6 (NKJV).

The Lord is telling us that we have an obligation to be bold in order to have a big harvest. God has entrusted us with His blessings of Liberty. Are you doing what you need to do to be a good steward of these blessings of Liberty?

Saint Paul said, *"We have different gifts . . . if your gift is . . . teaching then teach . . . if it is to lead, do it diligently"*—Romans 12: 6–8 (NIV).

I'm going to be bold and paraphrase Saint Paul and say: If you have the gift of teaching, then be a great teacher. If your gift is leading, then be a great leader. If your gift is supporting a leader, then be a great supporter. If your gift is writing, then be a great writer. If your gift is working in development and asking for major gifts, then be the best.

With this introduction, I hope you're encouraged to read on and see where you can best apply your talents—keeping in mind Christ's last words on earth as He ascended into heaven, *"Go ye therefore, and teach all nations . . ."* —Matthew 28:19 (KJV).

1

How It All Began

Growing up in Pasadena, Texas, playing cops and robbers, there was something I didn't tell the other kids. I wasn't shooting robbers; I was shooting Commies.

At age 16, I was going to bed about half of the nights listening to Harry Caray broadcast the St. Louis Cardinals games (at that time, the Cardinals were the most southern and western of all major league baseball teams) and the other half of the nights listening to the Rush Limbaughs of the late 1940s: John T. Flynn, Dan Smoot, or Fulton Lewis, Jr.

I have no recollection of any political conversation in my immediate or extended family, or any family friends talking about communism, politics, or anything dealing with national issues. I came into this world knowing communism is evil and dangerous, and I'll leave this world knowing the same.

In 1952, I was 19 and couldn't vote, but I was a Republican precinct chairman and manning a precinct for a presidential primary between Eisenhower and Taft (I was a Taft supporter) in Harris County (Houston). From 7 a.m. to 7 p.m., only two people showed up to vote that day, my mom and dad.

I later became chairman of the Harris County Young Republicans (YRs) and in 1960, Harris County chairman for John Tower for Senate. Tower was the Republican candidate for the U.S. Senate against Senator Lyndon Johnson, who was also on the ballot for vice president.

On a Saturday in June of 1961, I arrived at an army base outside of Chicago, Illinois, to fulfill my two-week requirement of active duty in the Army National Guard.

The following Saturday afternoon, everyone in my unit

7

went into town. I stayed in the barracks and, while reading Bill Buckley's *National Review*, I read in the classified ads section a one-inch ad for four field directors for Americans for Constitutional Action (ACA) run by retired Admiral Ben Moreell.

A week later, when I had returned home, I quickly called my friend David Franke, who was a writer at *National Review* and very active in conservative youth politics. I said to David, "I've got to have one of those four positions at ACA." He said, "It's not four, it's one. It was a blind ad to find a person to run Young Americans for Freedom (YAF)," which had been founded in September 1960 on Bill Buckley's family estate in Sharon, Connecticut. I immediately said, "David, get me that job." A few weeks later, I took the red eye to New York's LaGuardia Airport for a 10 a.m. Saturday morning interview with Bill Rusher, the long-time publisher of *National Review*.

After about 45 minutes, we took a cab to 79 Madison Avenue, NYC, where Marvin Liebman had his office. Marvin ran a small (six or seven employees) public affairs agency. YAF was a client of Marvin's, and they had their office in his agency.

Marvin was very close to Bill and Pat Buckley and spent most weekends with them in Sharon, Connecticut. Marvin had a number of conservative and anti-communist organizations as clients, including one he had founded and named "The Committee of 1,000,000 Against the Admission of Red China to the UN."

During the interview, Marvin showed me around his office, which included a mail room with a postage meter, envelopes, stationary, brochures, pamphlets, etc. But the most interesting thing was a large 3×5 card filing cabinet, which contained thousands of 3×5 index cards. Each one had a person's name, address, and the name of one or more organizations they had contributed to, usually because of an ad in a newspaper, such as the *Wall Street Journal* or the *New York Times*, with the amount and date of their donation.

To this day, I clearly remember thinking, "Wow, where has this thing been all my life?" I felt like a duck that had never seen water but knew what to do with the water.

Within days after I returned, Marvin offered me a job as an account executive at Marvin Liebman and Associates, handling the YAF account. Weeks later, the YAF Board of Directors (21 mostly college students, many from Ivy League schools like Harvard, Yale, Princeton, etc.) selected me to be YAF's executive secretary. A serious split had developed in YAF, but since my sponsors were David Franke, Bill Rusher, and Marvin Liebman representing Bill Buckley Jr., my selection was mostly a formality. Buckley, though only 36, was clearly the leader of the conservative movement and was already a god-like figure to conservatives, especially the youth.

So, in August of 1961, I left my job as a clerk in the land department of Western Natural Gas, making $90 a week, to go share an apartment in Greenwich Village with David Franke making $125 dollars a week.

One of the last things I did before I left Houston was to take my girlfriend, Elaine O'Leary, to the San Jacinto Monument and Battleground, about 30 miles east of Houston, and ask her to marry me. To my great fortune, she said yes, and I returned in mid-February to marry her.

I selected the San Jacinto battlegrounds for my proposal, because as a proud Texan and a traditionalist, I thought it would be cool to propose where General Sam Houston beat Santa Anna's Mexican army to win Texas's independence from Mexico.

When I arrived in New York on a Sunday afternoon, I was on cloud nine. I had a fiancée, and I was a junior officer on the front lines in the war for freedom, battling the American Left and the communists.

Monday, when I arrived at the YAF office, I was surprised to learn that YAF, which had a big national reputation, at just 11 months old had a debt of $20,000, only about 1,200 donors, and very little money coming in. One of my first assignments was to get in touch with three people Marvin suggested I call and ask for money: Charles Edison (former governor of New Jersey and youngest son of Thomas Edison), Captain Eddie Rickenbacker (a WWI hero and founder of Eastern Airlines), and J. Howard Pew (chairman of Sun Oil Company).

I called Edison and Rickenbacker on the phone and they both sent $1,000 checks. I went to Pittsburgh, Pennsylvania, to meet with Pew and we had a nice hour-long visit. Within weeks, $1,000 checks started to arrive from Pew and his family members for a total of $5,000.

However, I quickly learned I didn't personally like asking people for money. So, I started writing letters and that worked. Then I hired a secretary and purchased a mimeograph machine, which would print about 1,000 letters an hour. Soon, the $20,000 debt was paid, and money was flowing in.

In the spring of 1962, Marvin felt it was time for us to go off on our own. I moved the YAF office five or six blocks up Madison Avenue to the fourth floor of an office building with no elevator.

One afternoon, while sitting in my office, I looked up and there was 78-year-old Charles Edison, who'd walked 15 blocks from his apartment at the Waldorf Astoria Towers and up four flights of stairs to give us youngsters support and encouragement. He was a wonderful, kind, and generous man, a strong supporter of anti-communist and conservative causes. His main contact for public policy issues the last decade of his life was his friend Marvin Liebman.

In 1962, Robert Bauman, a U.S. House of Representatives page, replaced Robert Schuchman as chairman of YAF. Bauman wanted to move our offices to the Capitol Hill area of Washington, D.C. He would later serve four terms in the U.S. House of Representatives from Maryland.

That was fine with me, because the center of conservative politics was beginning to move to Washington, D.C. My 1960 U.S. Senate candidate, John Tower, was the newest U.S. Senator, having been elected in May 1961, in a special election to fill the vacancy created when Senator Lyndon Johnson resigned to become vice president.

Tower was the first Republican elected to the U.S. Senate from the old South since reconstruction. A draft Goldwater for President organization had recently been formed. Conservatives had founded a new political party in New York. YAF was doing battle daily on college campuses with the Left. Conservatives around the country were filled with energy and excitement.

In late 1962, YAF moved its national office into an office in the 500 block of C Street, NE. We had about six or seven employees, including myself and my secretary.

I was spending more and more time on direct mail. In the spring of 1963, I suggested to the YAF leadership that they bring a high school teacher, Florida YAF State Chairman David Jones, to Washington to run the organization, so that I could focus on direct mail and fundraising.

As previously mentioned, the YAF board was comprised mostly of college students or recent graduates from Harvard, Yale, Princeton, and other major colleges and universities. While I had graduated from the University of Houston and attended University of Houston Law School, I was not a good student.

In my first year at YAF, I often came into contact with Bill Buckley Jr., Brent Bozell Jr., Frank Meyer, Priscilla Buckley, James Burnham, Stan Evans, and other intellectual giants. I tried to make up for my lack of intellectual fire power by reading and studying, not only the writings of these conservative stars, but also Adam Smith, Edmund Burke, Whitaker Chambers, etc.

But after about a year, I realized I wasn't making a lot of progress. So, I made a conscious decision to stop reading the books and publications that I enjoyed and do a deep dive into the study of advertising/marketing/business.

My thinking was that while we conservatives didn't have enough writers, debaters, candidates, elected officials, or organizations, we did have some. But we had no one who could mass market our writers, books, magazines, candidates, and organizations, and lobby politicians, etc.

In 1963, I talked to my wife and said, "Honey, I've discovered something that's very important and it could help change America, maybe even the world. But I don't understand it, so I'll need to spend a lot of time studying. Can I be relieved of all household duties—no changing diapers, no taking out the trash, yard work, etc.? I need to spend all available time studying direct marketing."

She bought into it. Maybe I was a better salesman than I realized. So, for the next seven to eight years, I did a deep dive into the study of advertising, marketing, direct mail, and business.

Throughout my business career, Elaine has been a strong supporter, editor, and advisor. Unfortunately, she had a stroke in 2006. Her mind is fine, but it paralyzed her left side, causing her to need 24/7 care in an assisted living facility. The Lord has blessed us with three children and six grandchildren.

I estimate that in the last 60 years, I've spent over 45,000 hours studying marketing/business. In recent decades, I've reduced my study time to about two to three hours a day, six days a week.

David Franke, my New York City roommate before Elaine and I married, said I would walk around our apartment holding a copy of Pete Hoke's monthly magazine, *Reporter of Direct Mail*, and say, "David, direct mail is going to change American politics."

2

Viguerie's Four Horsemen
of Marketing®

I've developed a concept of marketing I've named VIGUERIE'S FOUR HORSEMEN OF MARKETING®.

There's little that's new or original about my Four Horsemen of Marketing®. I simply applied the principles I learned from spending 45,000 hours studying marketing, business, and direct mail in the last 60 years.

I drew upon the ideas of giants that have shared their wisdom with us, including Claude Hopkins, Rosser Reeves, John Caples, Ed Mayer Jr., Dick Benson, Al Ries, Jack Trout, Robert Cialdini, Seth Godin, and a dozen others.

The ideas of the Four Horsemen of Marketing can and should be applied to many areas of life, including getting into the college of your choice; marrying that pretty young lady who has numerous suitors; getting a job, promotion or raise; selling a product; raising money, etc., etc.

Here are my Four Horsemen of Marketing. To your audience, you must get all four right, and if you do, you will win. Get one wrong and you're not likely to succeed: *position, differentiation, benefit,* and *brand.*

I'm going to use the example of Rupert Murdoch starting a cable television channel, Fox Corporation, to illustrate my points.

First is *position.* The easiest way I know to think about position is it's a hole in the marketplace that is occupied by no one else—it's a private decision.

When Rupert Murdoch decided he wanted to launch a

cable television network, he didn't need to study CBS, NBC, or ABC. He brilliantly discovered a niche market that had been overlooked by others—half of the country—conservatives/Republicans.

America is a 50/50 country, half Republican, half Democrat. So, in the 1980s half of the country didn't have a TV channel they could go to and get the news, commentary, and information they wanted.

So, Murdoch privately decided to occupy that hole in the marketplace.

Second is *differentiation*, which is what you do publicly and visually to let people know your niche in the marketplace. Murdoch didn't take out ads that said Fox was a conservative TV network. He put forward, as the face of Fox News, people such as Bret Baier, Brit Hume, Glenn Beck, Megyn Kelly, Bill O'Reilly, Sean Hannity—later Tucker Carlson, Laura Ingraham, and Jesse Watters. You don't find people like them anywhere else on TV.

Third is *benefit*. What's the benefit someone personally receives by donating to your organization or using or buying your product?

Obviously, conservatives get news and information from Fox that they don't get from ABC, NBC, CBS, CNN, MSNBC, or public TV.

Fourth is *brand*. It's a combination of the first three (*position, differentiation,* and *benefit*). It's what makes you or your organization unique, one-of-a-kind—Seth Godin's "purple cow."

If you apply the Four Horsemen to MSNBC, they have a position, a differentiation, a brand, and (for liberals) a benefit, but they offer no benefit for conservatives.

These days, products are not sold, they are bought. People buy brands. They go with the leader. They may deny it—but they do it.

A few years ago, I wanted to replace my 13-year-old Lincoln with a Lexus. No one sold me on the idea of buying a Lexus. My wife had a Lexus, I liked it, and I wanted a two- to three-year-old black Lexus. All I had to do was find someone who would sell me a black Lexus at the price I wanted to pay. I did and that was four years ago, and one day I'll get another black Lexus.

People buy *brands*. Do you have a *brand*? Not if you don't own a category. In fact, *brand* is so important that I'm going to give it a chapter of its own—Chapter 3.

After you read about the Four Horsemen, you may feel you understand the concepts and you're ready to move on to something else. However, the odds are great you haven't mastered them. While the ideas seem simple, I've found very few people in marketing who truly understand them and even fewer who apply them correctly.

If you get one of the Four Horsemen wrong to the audience you're appealing to, you'll be going uphill with the wind in your face and unlikely to succeed. Get all four correct, and life will be downhill with the wind to your back and pushing you on your way to victory.

3

Brand Yourself, Brand Your Organization—Change Your Life, Change the World

In marketing, having a strong BRAND is not just a good or important thing to have—*it is the whole ballgame.*

Have you ever said or thought ...

> Why aren't we raising more money?
> Why don't we have more donors?
> Why don't we have more members?
> Why don't we have more subscribers?
> Why isn't our candidate higher in the polls?
> Why did we lose the election?
> Why isn't our organization better known?

or

Have you ever heard someone say ...

> Why didn't I get hired?
> Why didn't I get a promotion?
> Why didn't I get a raise?
> Why didn't she accept my marriage proposal? etc., etc.

It's a rare person, organization leader, or candidate who hasn't said some version of the above—perhaps many times.

And the answer often is that you, your organization, or candidate lacks a BRAND.

A high percentage of the time, the reason your nonprofit is stuck in size, money, members, subscribers, or not experiencing significant growth is because your BRAND is weak or non-existent.

I've learned that very few people truly understand what makes a BRAND. Even most people in marketing have little or no idea what constitutes a BRAND.

What's not a brand?

- We're smarter than the competition.
- We work more efficiently.
- We get more bang for the buck.
- We're a household name.
- We work harder.
- We get more results for less money.
- We're bigger, better.
- I (or our organization) am (is) famous and profitable.

Having a famous name or being well-known doesn't mean you have a BRAND. Having a successful business doesn't mean you have a BRAND. Does it matter if someone buys from you or a competitor? If not, then you don't have a BRAND.

Airlines such as United, Delta, and American do not have a BRAND. For myself and most Americans, it doesn't matter which airline we fly. We want to leave and arrive at a certain time, and the airline that best suits our schedule and budget is the one we fly.

In 2016, 17 people sought the Republican nomination for president. Today very few who follow politics can even remember half of them.

Think, what was the significant difference between Jeb Bush, Chris Christie, Bobby Jindal, John Kasich, Carly Fiorina, Rick Perry, or Marco Rubio? I couldn't begin to tell you the difference between them. It was not clear at all why GOP voters should select one rather than the other.

However, if you had asked any of the above candidates what separated them from the others, most would probably have said something to the effect of "I'm smarter than the others."

Sorry, the voters don't agree. To them, you're all smart or you wouldn't be on that stage.

Now you know what is not a BRAND—but what is a BRAND?

A BRAND is being the first in a new category and dominating that category. You want to "own" a category/project that's important to conservatives, and to position your organization as uniquely qualified to solve problem X.

Why is BRANDING important?

Because it creates a new category in the mind of a person. Once something is BRANDED, positive or negative, good or bad, it's like Super Glue—usually permanent.

Using myself as an example. My BRAND is I'm the pioneer of political/ideological direct mail. Our company in 1965 was the world's first political direct mail agency, and 57 years later, we're still the largest and best-known conservative direct mail agency.

For centuries people have been engaged in fundraising—churches, schools, politics; for many years organizations had been raising money through the mail for charities and other good causes. But no one had raised money for political candidates and ideological organizations through the mail. I started a new category raising ideological and political donations through postal mail.

In the 1980s, Congressman Jack Kemp organized a meet-and-greet visit with future Israeli Prime Minister Benjamin

Netanyahu for about 8–10 conservatives. Each one of us went around the conference table and just said our name. After I said Richard Viguerie, Netanyahu pointed at me and said, "Direct mail." Then and now, that is my BRAND—the pioneer of political direct mail.

Remember a BRAND is when you branch off from an existing category and start a new category. For example, 50 years ago there were three network TV channels: ABC, CBS, and NBC.

- Then a new category appeared—cable TV.
- Then a new category appeared—all news cable TV (CNN).
- Then a new category appeared—all sports cable TV (ESPN).
- Then a new category appeared—conservative cable TV (FOX).

So, if you want a BRAND, be the leader of a new category.

A successful BRANDING of a conservative organization will allow it to grow 100%–500%–1,000% in the next few years. Also, conservative candidates for public office need BRANDING. A law of politics is "Define [BRAND yourself] or be defined [your opponent will BRAND you]."

Read, read, study, study BRANDING and apply it to Democrats and to conservative organizations and save America. The single best book to learn about BRANDING is *The Origin of Brands* by Al and Laura Ries. Read the first 25 pages over and over until you really, really understand the concept of a BRAND.

This is not rocket science. We can do this people. We can save America.

4

Do You Have a Tagline?

Why am I devoting an entire chapter to something few people in marketing/communication ever think about? (And the few that do usually get it wrong.)

While a tagline is not "officially" part of the Four Horsemen, it probably should be.

Why is a tagline important?

Because your organization's name, business, or product usually doesn't describe who you are, what you do, why people give to you, buy from you, vote for you, etc. It doesn't say anything about who or what you are, or how you're different from others.

If you received a mailing from an organization named Voters for America, would you know if it was liberal or conservative? The same goes for Citizens for Honest Elections, or Action Now, or Listen America, or well . . . you get the point.

The purpose of a tagline is to let people quickly (one to two seconds) know they should pay attention because you're special, unique, one-of-a-kind, different from others. It must separate you from all others.

As Kathleen Patten, our company's president and CEO, says, "If your tagline can be accurately used by another, throw it away, keep thinking, keep writing until you have a tagline that works only for you."

A tagline is not, "We're the best," "We're better," or "We accomplish more for less."

While most good taglines are short (three to six words), don't overly worry about having a short, punchy tagline. Focus on having a good and effective tagline that separates you from all others.

Most ideological nonprofits do not have a name that identifies them as being on the right, left, or in the middle. How are people supposed to know if they agree with you or not unless they spend 5–10 minutes reading? And trust me, that seldom happens.

Most of us lead full and busy lives. We don't care to take time to try to figure out what you want, need, are selling, etc. On a really good day (and there are not many of them) you have about 10 seconds before your brilliant direct mail letter goes in the waste basket. However, on a typical day, you're lucky if you have five seconds.

And it's worse for emails. Many people get 50–100 a day. I get over 350. So you're looking at one or two seconds before they hit the delete button.

By the way, in a postal mailing, put the tagline in numerous places where it's most likely to be seen, including under the name of the organization, the bottom of the first page, the bottom of the last page, on the reply form, and any inserts.

Remember, the number one "secret" of advertising is repetition. Coca-Cola and Pepsi certainly know this.

Not only do most all organizations, candidates, and businesses need a tagline, but you personally would be helped if you identified how you wanted people to think of you in 5–10 words and started using it when speaking and/or writing.

I think all (even liberals) can agree that the most successful, best political tagline in decades is Donald Trump's "Make America Great Again"—MAGA. It set him apart from the other 16 GOP presidential candidates. It spoke to tens of millions of disillusioned, disappointed, upset, angry, forgotten Americans.

The Make America Great Again tagline played an important role in putting Donald Trump, who had never run for or held a public office, into the White House.

The problem is even greater with a candidate for public office than with a business or organization, because the candidate's name tells you nothing about their position on the issues, their values, opinions, beliefs, goals, etc.

A good tagline for a political candidate should give people a tune they can whistle. In my state of Virginia, recent successful Republican candidates for governor had effective taglines.

Virginia GOP Governors Gave the Voters a Tune to Whistle

1993	George Allen	You do the crime; you do the time
1997	Jim Gilmore	No Car Tax
2001	Bob McDonnell	Bob's for Jobs
2021	Glenn Youngkin	No Critical Race Theory taught in Virginia's schools

Most were years ago, and I remembered them without looking them up. They were "tunes you could whistle."

There are over a dozen good national pro-life organizations. But as active and involved as I am in the conservative movement, I have a difficult time understanding the difference between most of them.

An exception is "Students for Life." Their name alone separates them from all other pro-life groups. Also, the Four Horsemen of Marketing® (position, differentiation, benefit, and brand) is contained in their name. From their name, people can instantly recognize what they do and appreciate the benefit and importance of a young person speaking to another young person about life.

If people set your mailing aside to read later because they didn't immediately understand your request, there's an old saying you should remember: "A donation/sale delayed is usually a donation/sale lost."

Your tagline should make it crystal clear what your organization does, how you're unique/different, and why it's important for people/readers/donors, etc., to help you—because no one else does what you do.

Think of a tagline as the tail of an airplane. Just because it's at the end of the plane and doesn't get as much attention as the front or interior, doesn't mean it's not vitally important.

Without the tail of an airplane, it's not going to get airborne, much less fly at 30,000 feet. The same with your nonprofit. Without a good tagline, your wonderful marketing campaign may not get off the ground.

5

Brand Democrats and
Govern America

There is little, if anything, more important for conservatives to be doing than BRANDING Democrats as anti-American, anti-police, open-borders, and elite socialists/Marxists.

Throughout most of the twentieth century, Democrats successfully BRANDED Republicans as the party of the rich, big business, Wall Street, trickledown economics, etc. This BRANDING of the Republicans helped Democrats win many elections.

Now, it's conservatives' turn.

As the Democrats move hard and far left, conservatives have a once-in-a-century opportunity to BRAND them as being anti-God, anti-America, anti-police, soft on crime, open-borders, elite, socialists/Marxists, and that BRAND could prevent them from winning national elections for decades to come (White House, control of U.S. Senate/U.S. House).

However, for conservatives to effectively BRAND the Democrats as stated above, we need to do five big things:

1. **Brand Democrats** in a MACRO way (nationally).
2. **Brand Democrats** in a MICRO way (to categories of voters).
3. **Connect Democrats to America's Problems**. Avoid referring to people as big city mayors, progressive prosecutors, defund the police politicians. All of these should be identified as who/what they are—*democrats*.

      When you speak or write about Joe Biden, Nancy Pelosi, Chuck Schumer, AOC, The Squad, etc., be sure to identify them as *democrats*. The importance of connecting *democrats* to America's problems is that on the ballot, people are identified as Democrats, not liberals/progressives/socialists, or Republicans, not conservatives.

4. **Educate Family, Friends, and Neighbors.** Educate, engage, encourage, empower, and activate 25, 50, or 100 of your family, friends, and neighbors. Then when millions of grassroots conservative activists do the same, it will lead to educating over 100 million voters. Then, conservatives will govern America for decades, perhaps generations.

5. **Be the Leader You Are Looking For.** Read on . . .

If millions of conservatives become modern-day political Paul Reveres, we will be so successful in BRANDING the Democrats that they may have to abandon the Democrat name and form a new political party.

Now back to Number 5 above. It's probably the most important thing of all: *you* and *your leadership*.

As our beloved Ronald Reagan used to say, "If not us, who? If not now, when?"

Obviously, we can't depend on Big Media—most all have joined with the progressive/socialist/Marxist Democrats

And the same for Big Tech (Google, Facebook, YouTube, etc.).

As if that's not bad enough, we also can't depend on the Republican Party and most national Republican politicians, because too many are weak, boneless, and spineless in fighting Democrats. Also, most national and state GOP committees and politicians are under the control and/or influence of content-free Republican consultants.

There are many good sources on the web where you will find current news articles, videos, editorials, conservative articles, e-books, news articles, etc., to forward to others, including FedUpPAC.org, ConservativeHQ.org, LeadershipInstitute.org, Heritage.org, HeritageAction.com, Newsmax.com, and WesternJournal.com. There is a larger list in Appendix 2.

If our BRANDING is effective, between now and 2024, some of the "older/wiser" Democrats will be holding meetings in early 2025 to discuss abandoning today's Democrat Party to the socialists/Marxists (Pelosi, Schumer, AOC, MSNBC, CNN) and forming a new "mainstream" political party.

As I said, we need to BRAND Democrats in two ways: macro (to all voters) and micro (to categories of voters).

Macro—Our BRANDING will be effective because most Americans are patriots who love our country. The big issues where the Democrats have moved far left are well known; however, you may find a partial review helpful.

BRAND DEMOCRATS MACRO—TO ALL VOTERS

Defund the police – Joe Biden

In a TV interview (*NowThis News*), host Ady Barkan asked Biden, "Can we agree that we can redirect some of the funding [from the police]?" Biden replied, "Yes, absolutely" (*NowThis News*, July 8, 2020). President Biden has been joined by many national, state, and local Democrats calling for and working to cut police budgets, which is seriously hurting police morale and allowing an increase in crime.

We must make sure the Democrats, in the public's mind, own the "defund the police" movement.

Street crime must continue – Kamala Harris

When asked about rioters that are destroying American cities, Kamala Harris said, "They're not going to stop. And everyone beware—because they're not going to stop. They're not going to stop before Election Day in November [2020], and they're

not going to stop after Election Day. And that should be—
everyone should take note of that, on both levels, that they're
not going to let up, and they should not, and we should not"
(*The Late Show with Stephen Colbert,* June 18, 2020).

Open borders

During the first Democrat presidential debate on June 26,
2019, Biden said that when he is president, illegal immigrants
should "immediately surge to the border."

Democrats are opening wide our southern border to illegals (including dangerous criminals), which drives up welfare
costs and causes high unemployment as illegals flood the job
market and work cheaper. Democrats' open-border policy is
also bringing in hundreds of thousands of COVID-positive
illegals. The Biden administration is sending them throughout
America.

Soft on crime

"Defunding the police isn't radical, it's real" —Tweet from
Democrat Congresswoman Cori Bush on January 28, 2021.

"We have seen video after video over the last few weeks
of peaceful protesters being met with extreme violence from
police. We can't wait. It's time to overhaul our policing system"
—Tweet from Democrat Congresswoman Barbara Lee on June
5, 2020.

In 2020, the Democrat majority on the Philadelphia City
Council gave approval to cut $33 million from the police
department. Now, "Philadelphia is on pace to have one of its
deadliest years [2021] on record" —NBC10 Philadelphia.

In Portland, Oregon, Democrat city commissioners cut
nearly $16 million from the police in June 2020 (Associated
Press, June 17, 2020). Portland Police Association Executive
Director Daryl Turner warned during an appearance on *NBC
Nightly News* in late June 2021 that officer morale is "as bad as

it's ever been" as the Democrat-run city experiences a sharp rise in violent crime.

Democrats have a long history of being soft on crime and criminals. Democrat governors, mayors, and prosecutors are letting hardened criminals out of jail and refusing to prosecute many crimes, including shoplifting, which encourages more crime and the destruction of small businesses.

Critical Race Theory (CRT)

CRT is a racist, mean, and evil attempt by Democrats to indoctrinate our children and adults that all whites are racists, minorities are victims being held down by whites, and America, the greatest country in the history of the world, is racist to its core.

Sky high gas prices

The Democrats are warring against fossil fuels (oil and gas), including cancelling the Keystone XL Pipeline and forbidding more drilling on federal lands. This is causing sky-high gas and oil prices and is a big gift to Russian dictator Putin, whose economy is strongly tied to the oil and gas he sells to Europe.

Inflation

Inflation is the direct result of the Democrats spending $7 trillion in 2021 to buy votes and turn America into a one-party, socialist/Marxist country. By putting massive amounts of money into the economy, but not increasing the supply of goods, more dollars began chasing a limited amount of goods and services—thereby driving up the cost of most everything.

Changing election laws to keep Democrats permanently in power

Democrats oppose asking people for an ID to vote, insist on keeping non-voters on the voting rolls, support mailing everyone in the government database a ballot (those with multiple name spellings and addresses will get multiple ballots), promote voting six weeks before Election Day for no reason, which means we no longer have Election Day—we have election season. Some Democrats even favor allowing illegal aliens, as well as 16- and 17-year-olds, to vote, etc.

Erase all differences between males and females, including girls/women's sports

Democrats say people should be able to declare themselves any of 57 different genders, which will destroy the culture of America, including girls' and women's sports.

And as you know, there are dozens more issues, which will BRAND the Democrats, including sexualizing school children, high taxes, out-of-control government spending that leads to runaway inflation, packing/destroying the Supreme Court, D.C. and Puerto Rican statehood, etc., etc.

BRAND DEMOCRATS MICRO—TO CATEGORIES OF VOTERS

Most people are normal. They are not like some of us, attending political meetings in the middle of the week, or on a Saturday morning going door-to-door. However, for most voters, there are one or two, maybe even three, issues that are so important that they trump all other issues. And on that issue, they will become activists, attending meetings, making phone calls, etc. By stressing these issues of particular concern to an interest group, it can increase the conservative/Republican vote by three to five points from each group of voters.

And when you increase each interest group's vote for Republicans by even a few percentage points, Republicans will start winning elections by landslide numbers.

Go Hunting Where the Voters Are
Some examples of important voting categories

- **Parents**
  - CRT—teaching our children that all whites are racist and all people of color are victims.
  - Democrat-led teachers unions want to sexualize five-, six-, and seven-year-olds, including telling them they can change from being a boy to being a girl, or that a girl can become a boy.
  - Democrats say you are a bigot and a mean person if you don't approve of a biological male calling himself a female and participating in women's sports and using women's bathrooms and showers.

- **Gun Owners**
  - Licensing, restricting, and taking away Second Amendment rights.

- **Seniors**
  - Security—Democrats want to defund the police.
  - Security—Democrats refuse to stop street violence and prosecute the law breakers.

- **Single Women**
  - Security—Democrats want to defund the police.
  - Security—Democrats refuse to stop street violence and prosecute the law breakers.

- **African Americans**
  - Education—Democrats oppose charter schools.
  - Education—Democrats oppose school choice.

- **Hispanics**
  - Jobs—Democrats are destroying their hopes for achieving the "American Dream" with illegal immigration and the inability to get work at a good wage.

- **Evangelicals**
  - Democrats are anti-God and anti-religion.
  - Abortion—Democrats want abortion-on-demand at any time and any reason.

- **Catholics**
  - Democrats are anti-God and anti-religion.
  - Abortion—Democrats want abortion-on-demand at any time and any reason.

- **Millennials**
  - Democrats want to abolish privacy with new regulations, increased personal tracking, automobile tracking, forced vaccinations, medical passports, and teaming up with Big Tech to track your whereabouts in your car, through smartphones, GPS apps, etc.

Because the leadership of every major American institution and government agency supports progressive/socialist/Marxist policies, conservatives must counter that by millions of grassroots activists becoming modern-day Paul Reveres and BRAND these people as Democrats. The Democrat BRAND will then become so toxic that conservative Republicans will govern America far into the future.

By the way, using the term "woke" is not helpful in BRANDING the Democrats. It doesn't label the Democrats as having dangerous beliefs, views, and values. If, instead of calling

Democrats "woke," we refer to them as anti-American social-ists/Marxists, that will be a highly toxic BRAND. I feel the same way about the term "politically correct." It doesn't have any negative connotation to most people.

6

Newt's Four-Part Plan

My heritage is Cajun. Ask a Cajun chef how to prepare any Cajun dish, and he or she will each start with the same sentence, "Well, first you make a roux [a sauce]." My advice before starting any important project is, "Well, first you start with what I call 'Newt's Four-Part Plan.'"

For about 10 years (mid-1970s to mid-1980s), seven or eight national conservative leaders would come to our home in McLean, Virginia, from 7:30 to 9:30 every Wednesday morning for a two-hour breakfast meeting: Paul Weyrich, Ed Feulner, Terry Dolan, Howard Phillips, Morton Blackwell, Ron Godwin (president of Moral Majority), and others.

When others of our national conservative colleagues and friends would be in town, they would frequently join us for breakfast.

Then for a while in the early 1980s, we would re-convene in the evening for a three-hour dinner with the same people as breakfast, but we would be joined by six or seven mostly young congressmen: Newt Gingrich, Vin Weber, Bob Walker, Hal Daub, Bill Dannemeyer, and a few others. To the extent that there was ever anything like what Hillary Clinton called a "Vast Right-wing Conspiracy," these breakfasts and dinners would have been it.

Each Wednesday evening as we strategized to build the conservative movement, some problem, opportunity, or need would arise, and Newt Gingrich would go to the blackboard (we didn't have whiteboards in those days) and write five words in four categories. Thirty minutes later, when we had filled in the four categories, we would see a clear path forward.

Newt's Four-Part Plan

1. Vision
2. Goal
3. Strategy
4. Tactics/Projects

Now, this is not the only way to write a plan, but it is a good simple template. And keep in mind that the most important part of the plan is not working the plan. That's important, but it's secondary to writing the plan, because as you think and write the plan, ideas come into focus and you begin to see more clearly when, where, and how to go forward with what you need to add to your life, leave behind, change, abandon, etc. Writing the plan helps clarify/crystalize your thinking. I do this one or two times a week, before important meetings, phone calls, prepping for a trip, etc. What's the purpose of the meetings, trips, phone calls? What's my number one goal for the meeting? What's my number two goal? Who do I want to meet with at the conference? Etc.

The premier business consultant of the twentieth century, Peter Drucker, said, "Culture eats strategy for breakfast." And Kevin Gentry in his weekly blog, *Tips*, on March 5, 2022, quotes his friend and mentor, Dino Cortopassi: "The best tactics or operations in the world with a so-so strategy can only take you so far. But a superior strategy, even with mediocre tactics, can fly you to the moon."

In our breakfasts and dinners, we were strategizing how to build the conservative movement and effectively battle the Left. In June of 1975, John Filka of the *Washington Star* wrote an article and referred to us as the "New Right." That phrase caught on. We were clearly new and different conservatives.

The New Right was the same ideologically as the Old Right;

however, we were operationally different. We would start our day thinking about what two, three, four things we could do today to advance the conservative cause and liberty, and defeat liberals. Also, the New Right (unlike the Old Right), as well as today's conservatives, included social/cultural issues as part of our agenda.

The Old Right, personified by conservative giants like Senators Bob Taft, Barry Goldwater, Strom Thurmond, and John Tower, would show up for a vote in Congress, get beat 2-1, and ask, "When's the next vote?" When told, they would say something like, "Ok, I'll be back." In other words, as Morton Blackwell said after he had been in Washington, D.C., a year or two, it came as a great shock when he realized Barry Goldwater, Strom Thurmond, John Tower, and other conservative politicians did not meet once a day, once a week, once a month, or even once a year to plan conservative strategy.

In those days, no one was leading the conservative movement. I sometimes describe the conservatives after Goldwater's 1964 loss and before Reagan's 1980 election to the presidency as conservatives being leaderless. It was like my friends and I were sitting in the back of an airplane that was going through a lot of turbulence. The plane was bouncing all over the sky. So, Weyrich, Phillips, Feulner, Falwell, Blackwell, Dolan, Phyllis Schlafly, Paul Laxalt, Jesse Helms, Tom Ellis, and others, and I got up our courage, walked to the front of the plane, and knocked on the cockpit door. (You could do that in the 1970s.) There was no answer, so we opened the door and found it empty—no one was flying the plane.

In other words, no one was in charge of the conservative movement.

We all began to take our seats, got out our legal pads, put down our coffee cups, picked up a copy of *Human Events, National Review, Conservative Digest,* and began a seven- to eight-year process of leading the conservative movement.

That lasted until January 1981 when Ronald Reagan was sworn in as the fortieth president of the United States, and of course he became the leader of the conservative movement.

The Old Right operated as a two-legged stool, which is not very sturdy. The two legs of the stool were economic issues (lower taxes, balanced budgets, etc.) and national security (which mostly meant anti-communism). However, under the leadership at first of Paul Weyrich and Jerry Falwell, conservatives began to add traditional values issues to the country's political discussion, and now conservatives were sitting on a three-legged stool. And by the late 1970s, instead of getting 45, 47, or 48% of the vote, conservatives started to get 51, 52, even 55% of the vote.

I strongly encourage conservative organizations to have:

- a three- to five-year big picture plan for their organization,
- a plan to double their donors in the next 12 to 18 months, and
- a plan to grow their organization by 10× in the next three to five years.

Most people think of a plan as a list of their dreams, wishes, hopes, aspirations, etc.

"I want to get a good paying job" is not a plan, it's a goal.
"I want a wife" is not a plan, it's a goal.
"I want to be a millionaire by age 30" is not a plan, it's a goal.
"I want to raise $10 million this year" is not a plan, it's a goal.
"I want to get 55% of the vote" is not a plan, it's a goal.

Few conservative organizations have a written plan for the next three years, two years, or even this year. Without a well-written plan, it will be difficult to raise high dollar/major donations, because wealthy donors can see you don't have the foggiest idea how to go from A to B, much less A to Z.

Winston Churchill said, "Plans are of little importance, but planning is everything."

As the old saying goes, "If you don't know where you're going, any train or road will get you there."

7

Needed: 20,000 New Single-Issue Conservative Organizations

As I've previously written, liberals have about 20,000 single-issue grassroots organizations, and conservatives have about 1,000–2,000.

If you find that hard to believe, consider just one category of liberal groups: unions. All major unions have not only a national office (usually in Washington, D.C.) but most have offices in each state. And many have offices in all large cities and counties. So unions, such as electricians' unions, will have hundreds of offices throughout the 50 states, counties, cities.

Multiply the number of electrician unions by the same number for the autoworkers, truck drivers, carpenters, pipe fitters, teachers, college professors, firefighters, meatcutters, teamsters, steel workers, machinists, welders, postal workers, and the national, state, and local level government employees, and you can quickly see with just unions that there are over 5,000 liberal organizations dedicated to the election of Democrats.

Issues Democrats Used to Build 20,000 Organizations

- Abortion
- Peace
- War
- Students
- Religion
- Separation of church and state

- Veterans
- Election reform
- Civil rights
- Children
- Elder advocacy
- Disability rights
- Women issues
- LGBT
- Immigration
- Illegal immigration
- Reparations
- Gun control
- Ending hunger
- Law enforcement
- Criminal justice
- Environmental
- Population control
- Business regulation
- Health issues
- Welfare

Twenty thousand new single-issue conservative organizations are needed at the local, state, and national levels.

Ideas for New Conservative Organizations

- Genocide/persecution of Christians in the Middle East, China, etc.
- School choice
- Stop indoctrination of school children
- Stop sexualizing school children
- Election integrity
- Veterans' well being
- Supporting good law enforcement

- Stop defund the police efforts
- Stopping abuse of power by the Intelligence Community
- Overregulation of small business
- Overregulation of private property
- Border control
- Religious liberty
- National Security (this issue can move single women to vote Republican)
- Seniors
- Oppose Medicare for all (it will destroy seniors' healthcare)
- No socialized medicine (it will lead to rationing of healthcare for all, especially seniors)
- Choice in education (will have a strong appeal to Black and Hispanic mothers)
- Reform of the criminal justice and prison system (if conservatives don't lead, it won't happen, as liberals are understandably afraid to get out in front on this issue)
- Hispanics for border control
- Reform of the administrative state
- Defunding the Left
- Protecting free speech and defeating censorship of conservatives
- Educating about the Constitution and our founding principles
- Opposing the U.N. and other transnational organizations that seek to destroy American sovereignty
- American energy independence
- Term limits
- Defeating socialism in America
- Community safety
- Respecting Judeo-Christian values
- De-politicizing the military

- Challenging woke corporations and institutions and their leaders
- Defeating soft-on-crime prosecutors
- Exposing climate fraud
- Protecting Right to Work
- Jobs/entrepreneurship (make it far easier to start a small business—less red tape)
- Catholics (brand Democrats as anti-God, anti-Catholic, party of abortion on demand)
- Evangelicals (brand Democrats as anti-God, anti-Evangelical, party of abortion on demand)
- Abortion (brand Democrats as the party of abortion on demand until moment of birth)

Since the Civil War, Catholics have voted Democrat about 55% of the time and GOP 45%. In 2008, Obama carried the Catholic vote by 9 points. In 2012, Obama carried the Catholic vote by just 2 points. In 2016, Trump carried the Catholic vote by 7 points, 52–45. That's a change of 9 points from 2012. The Catholic vote is a major reason Trump carried Pennsylvania, Michigan, and Wisconsin in 2016 and won the presidency (Americamagazine.org, "How Have Catholics Voted in Past Elections?" Oct. 3, 2020; Pew Research Center, "8 Facts about Catholics and Politics)".

If Catholics start voting in the range of 55% Republican, it will be very difficult for Democrats to win the White House or control Congress. Remember, the Catholic vote is concentrated in purple and blue states. This can be a game changer.

Of course, it's important to keep the Evangelical vote at 80+%.

If Barack Obama called a meeting of all liberal national environmental nonprofits, there would be 300–350 groups represented. However, if Dr. Kevin Roberts, president of the Heritage Foundation, called for a meeting of all conservative/

free-market environmental groups—at most there would be five or six organizations represented.

Most Americans have little or no interest in politics. They're focused on their families, education, jobs, hobbies, finding a spouse, planning a weekend trip, etc. They have no interest in attending a political meeting this evening, making a donation to a political party, attending a rally for a political candidate, or putting up a political yard sign or a bumper sticker on their car.

However, as I said in Chapter 5, for most everyone there are one or two, maybe even three, issues that they will leave home for to go to a Tuesday night meeting or a Saturday morning rally.

Maybe the issue is their children's failed public school or the local school board indoctrinating their children with Critical Race Theory. Or the local district attorney is failing to protect the community from repeat criminals. Or the mayor and city council are over-taxing and over-regulating their family's small business. Or the governor and/or state legislators are infringing on their religious liberty.

In 1964, Hillary Rodham (Clinton) was a Goldwater Girl. But by 1969, she was a hard-core leftist, and it had nothing to do with the Democrat Party. Hillary Rodham became a liberal almost overnight because of one issue: opposition to the Vietnam War.

Think about the issues that people in your neighborhood, community, town, or county are talking about. What are your family, friends, and neighbors upset about?

I'll use Critical Race Theory (CRT) as an example.

If you discover that CRT is being taught in your local public school, identify six to eight people you know in your community who share your views and values. Invite them over for coffee/tea and doughnuts on a Saturday morning. Tell them you want to talk about CRT indoctrinating the children in your local public school. After you spend time "cussing" the problem, suggest a committee or a task force be formed, and propose someone to be the leader.

Next, suggest a larger meeting in a week or two of maybe 25 to 30 in someone's living room, basement, or backyard. At the larger meeting, discuss possible next steps that could include 1) calling for a big turnout at the next school board meeting, 2) committing to finding candidates to run in the next school board election, city council, state legislative race, or 3) perhaps even organizing a much larger meeting with topflight speakers, etc.

You'll need people to volunteer for projects, including organizing the next meeting, candidate recruitment, media, and maybe someone to be in charge of fundraising, legal advice, etc.—which will greatly expand your leadership team.

Nothing moves that's not pushed. Perhaps the number one quality you're seeking in leaders is energy—someone with an entrepreneurial/risk-taking spirit. Too many conservative leaders have low energy.

You may want to keep the group, especially in the early stages, informal—not a legal entity. Politicians have written laws to make it more difficult to challenge their agenda. Also, consider including in the group a local attorney who shares your views and values.

By starting a new organization focused on a single issue, you're forming what I call a third-force organization—you're independent of the Republican and Democrat parties.

I consider myself not a Republican, but a limited government constitutional conservative who operates within the Republican Party.

Third-force nonprofits have their own members, agenda, money, and issues. They're completely separate from all political parties. Their mission is to pull all political parties, politicians, and public opinion toward their viewpoint.

Think how the Left operates. The unions, environmental groups, race-based organizations, social justice groups, etc., all operate independent of the Democrat Party, and each has their own source of money, members, and their own agenda. Each one is trying to pull the country to the Left.

By the way, as a general rule, the largest nonprofits are those focused on one issue. Those that deal with lots of different issues have a hard time getting people's attention. The largest right-of-center organization is focused on one issue. You may have guessed, it's the NRA (National Rifle Association), and their issue is the Second Amendment.

Perhaps you've heard this, "You may not be interested in war, but war is interested in you."

I'll paraphrase that and say, "You may not be interested in politics, but politics is interested in you." These days, politicians want more of your money in taxes, want to reduce your freedoms, close your church, take your guns, force vaccinations, open borders, and bring in illegal aliens with COVID and criminal records and place them in your neighborhood.

Conservatives, we're close to losing our Constitution, our liberties, and our country to the enemies of freedom under God's laws—the socialists/Marxists.

Today America needs you to be one of three million conservatives who can do one or more of the following:

Where Can You Help?

- Help educate 25, 50, or 100 of your family, friends, neighbors that Democrats are mean, evil, anti-American, elite socialists/Marxists.
- Start a new conservative organization.
- Help someone who starts a new conservative organization.
- Help an existing conservative organization.

- Be a candidate for one of the 519,682 elected offices, if they are not occupied by an effective conservative.
- Help someone who steps forward as a candidate.
- Help an incumbent conservative official be re-elected.

At age 89, God has blessed me with good health and lots of energy, allowing me to spend 65 hours a week answering the call He gave to Isaiah, "Who will go for me?" "Here I am, Lord, send me."

How about you? Will you answer God's call today? America is worth an hour a day. We have no right to drop the torch of liberty lit by America's Founders, so that those who come after us (including our children and grandchildren) will be enslaved by an all-powerful, socialist/Marxist government.

8

How and Why to Acquire New Donors

Direct mail is still the workhorse to raise money and acquire new donors for conservative nonprofits.

This is true of ideological fundraising on the left and right, as well as health, welfare, and other nonprofits. My friend of over 45 years, Roger Craver, who did the pioneering direct mail work for liberals and is still the leading authority for Leftists on direct marketing in 2022, said that of the four major ways people raise money from the new and alternative media (direct mail, digital, phones, TV), 90% still comes from direct mail.

This will change, but not for many years.

Without the post office and direct mail, there would be no conservative movement worthy of the name. Find that hard to believe?

Few right-of-center organizations are as good at marketing/fundraising as the world-class people at the Heritage Foundation. Heritage rightly prides itself on spending significant time and energy on helping other conservative organizations, including sharing helpful information.

See Chapter 19, where I identify 11 big mistakes conservative leaders make. In number six, I discuss the importance of low-dollar donors to the Heritage Foundation becoming the world's largest think-tank.

A few years ago, at a marketing meeting for a large conservative organization, someone asked Christy Fogarty, a former marketing executive at Heritage, what was the number one thing she would do differently, if she could relive her time at Heritage. Her immediate answer was, "Mail more."

I believe only a few conservative organizations spend enough money on the acquisition of new donors, members, and supporters. However, the size of conservative organizations matters greatly. Large conservative organizations with big budgets and big bank accounts are necessary to compete and win against the Left's dozens of giant organizations.

So why does the Left have dozens of nonprofits with 100,000+ supporters, but there are only a few on the right?

I've seen the inside of more conservative nonprofit organizations than any living or deceased conservative. Here are a few reasons why conservative organizations have so few donors compared to liberals.

Most Conservative Organization Leaders:

- Fear failure.
- Have low energy.
- Lack money to invest in growth and don't know how to acquire the money.
- Feel it's too expensive. ("I tried it once and lost money.")
- Are hesitant to invest scarce dollars now to achieve an unseen long-term benefit.
- Know they and their team lack the professional skills to conduct a large direct mail campaign.
- Fear growth. If an organization's donors grow from 10,000 to 200,000, the leadership responsibility, work, stress, and pressure increase significantly, but their salary doesn't increase correspondingly.
- Go into the future facing the past. They are confidently doing things the way they've done them for 5, 20, or 40 years, and it's uncomfortable/scary to turn around and face the future. Being bold and aggressive for the first time in their life is out of their comfort zone.

Human nature being what it is, if conservatives are ever to be competitive with the Left in grassroots marketing, it will be done mostly by those under 40 years old.

God, in His infinite wisdom, seldom saw fit to put an entrepreneurial spirit in a nonprofit executive. A high percentage of executives went into the nonprofit world for the same reason many people go into government: they don't like the competition, stress, and pressure that you find in the highly competitive business world.

If you work for a national conservative organization, the chances are your opponents on the Left have about 700% more donors and probably raise about 700% more money than you do.

It's shocking that this is so when you consider that most all crises and problems facing Americans are caused by the policies and programs of the Left, including failed public schools, schools that teach immorality, schools that teach that whites are racists and minorities are victims, high taxes, massive government debt, out-of-control government spending leading to high inflation, defund the police movements, crime, invasion by illegals because of an open southern border, promotion of socialism, etc., etc.

The only explanation I can offer is that most conservative leaders have low energy and lack leadership skills, and therefore are ineffective.

Again, to repeat Kevin Gentry, "The lack of experimentation and risk-taking is maddening. Have our folks lost the will to win?" I don't know of any other reason why conservatives have about 1,000–2,000 single-issue organizations and 3 to 4 million donors, but liberals have 20,000 organizations and 21 million+ individual donors.

In the 1960s–80s, conservatives had many more grassroots supporters/donors than liberals. How can conservative nonprofits greatly increase the number of their donors and once again compete and perhaps dominate in grassroots marketing?

Want a Big, Successful Organization? Do These Things:

1. Read and study the information in this book, especially Chapter 19: "11 Big Mistakes Conservative Leaders Make."

2. Put someone in charge of your organization's marketing, so they "own" your direct marketing fundraising program, including the results. Make sure that the person becomes an expert in marketing by reading, reading, and studying, studying the giants of direct mail and fundraising (see Direct Marketing/Fundraising Suggested Reading in Appendix 1). Courage will be needed by conservative leaders to significantly grow their organizations, including raising massive amounts of money.

3. Before you start to write a letter, be sure you have your audience clearly in mind. Of course, you write to seniors differently than middle-age pro-life supporters, small business owners, parents with young children, etc.

4. Develop projects that will appeal to the audience you're writing to. The projects should be specific with a price tag, a start date, a finish date, and provide a significant benefit to the donor and America.

5. Make sure your projects fit the mailing lists. For example, when writing to lists of small-business owners, you want to have different projects than when you write to people on religious or seniors' lists.

6. Develop mailing programs/letters to categories of lists beyond the 3 or 4 million existing conservative donors. There are many categories of lists of potential donors you should be testing/mailing, e.g., religious, sports,

business, charities, seniors, law enforcement, and veterans. At ATA, we call that "going out of market."

If conservative organizations only appeal to the existing conservative donors, we will not increase the number of conservative donors and never beat the Left with their 21 million+ donors. Especially now when the Democrat Party has lurched so far to the Marxist Left, there are millions of Americans who are more open to the conservative message about values we know are eternal.

7. Another important reason to go out of the conservative market is you'll be getting donors that are not being bombarded with appeals from 100+ other conservative groups, and that also means you will have less competition for major gifts, wills, and bequests.

8. Here's a mistake most conservative nonprofit organizations make: "Send me money because Democrats are doing bad things." I call this writing "cuss letters." Yes, you can raise money by simply telling people that Democrats are causing this or that problem, but you'll raise a great deal more money if you also tell the potential donor how you are going to solve that problem if you raise X dollars for Y and Z projects.

9. Look for a hungry market. A famous direct marketer, Gary Halbert, said, "Don't focus on making a better hamburger, look for a hungry market." In other words, when it's feasible, focus on solving problems that people are well aware of and worried about.

10. Seek major donors who will contribute the money needed to finance the building of a large list of donors.

11. Invest in your marketing team's education and training. Seek out conferences, seminars, and masterminds for them to learn from.

12. Hire young people with ambition and energy, train

them, and give them a reason to make a career by continuing to work for you. I regularly hear people say, "I can't find good people," and I reply, "Tell me why a talented, bright, ambitious young person should come and work for your organization." That usually causes them to focus on how they're appealing to prospective employees.

13. When mailing to acquire new donors, avoid asking for a lot of money. First get your foot in the door, then establish a relationship. There's plenty of time to upgrade their giving level. Remember two-thirds of Heritage major donors started with a low dollar donation to a postal mailing. Socialist/Democrat presidential candidate Bernie Sanders developed a file of 2 million unique donors and the first request was always for only $2.70.

9

A Scary Look at Liberal Dark Money and Grassroots Marketing

In 1961, when I started using direct mail to market conservative organizations, candidates, and causes, not only did conservatives not use the mail, but neither did the Left.

Liberals in the 1960s and '70s received most of their money from three sources: unions, foundations, and the government (you, the taxpayer). Today, the Left receives tens of billions of dollars annually from those three sources, but they also receive tens of billions from multi-millionaires and billionaires, especially Big Tech billionaires, Hollywood, and Fortune 500 companies and their executives, etc.

There is not one conservative major donor who comes close to being a Mark Zuckerberg, who contributed $417 million in 2020 to dozens of liberal organizations to increase the Democrat vote. In addition to Zuckerberg, Democrats have many mega donors including George Soros, Jeff Bezos, McKenzie Scott (Jeff Bezos's former wife), Mike Bloomberg, Tom Steyer, and Bill Gates.

Consider the fact that Democrat Jeff Bezos spent $250 million personally to buy the leftwing *Washington Post* in 2013 and then spends many millions of dollars each year to grow, expand, and subsidize the paper's losses (see Appendices 5 and 6).

However, as important as the massive amount of money the Left receives from the above sources, perhaps the most important source of money is from the 21+ million grassroots donors who give $2, $5, $10, $25, $50, $100, or $200 to liberal causes.

As I've said before, the Left raises about 700% more grassroots money than conservatives from about 700% more donors.

And of course, when you contribute money to a liberal organization that greatly increases the chances you will vote Democrat. Also, because you're financially invested in a cause, you probably will talk about it to your family, friends, neighbors, and others.

The Left has about 20,000 single-issue organizations whose purpose is to massively expand government, elect Democrats, give power to unelected bureaucrats, and reduce the liberty, freedom, and power of citizens. My research indicates that conservatives only have about 1,000–2,000 single-issue nonprofits.

The 20,000 liberal organizations will each need a president, vice president, and secretary/treasurer, as well as vice presidents of fundraising, membership, media, special events, etc. The way you become a leader is by leading, so when the liberals have 20,000+ ideological organizations each with five to seven officers/leaders that gives them over 100,000 liberals training to be future candidates for school board, city council, state legislature, Congress, etc.

Of the 30 ideological nonprofits with the largest budgets, only seven are conservative and 23 are liberal.

The 100 largest liberal nonprofits in 2019 had income of $46,446,445,444, while the 100 largest conservative nonprofits had income of $8,078,932,107. Conservatives have another 900 nonprofits that received income to advance the conservative cause, but liberals have income from another 19,900 nonprofits to advance their socialist agenda. In Appendix 5 and 6, there are lists of the 100 largest conservative and 100 largest liberal nonprofits by income.

One liberal organization alone, ActBlue, in the 2019–20 election cycle raised $4.3 billion from 13.4 million individual liberals who gave them their credit card information to make quick and easy donations to liberal candidates and nonprofits.

In the introduction, I wrote that when Donald Trump was elected president in November 2016, Planned Parenthood had 400,000 supporters—12 months later they had 1.6 million. In addition to Planned Parenthood, there are many other left-wing groups promoting the killing of over 1 million babies a year, including:

- Guttmacher Institute (2019 Income: $24,255,758)
- NARAL Pro-Choice America (2019 Income: $12,400,056)
- National Network of Abortion Funds
  (2020 Income: $20,343,642) (National and 27 affiliates)
- Center for Reproductive Rights
  (2020 Income: $38,755,766)
- Plus, 183 other pro-abortion groups (see Appendix 6)

In 2020, 188 pro-abortion groups had income of $3.4 billion (LifeNews.com, "Pro-Abortion Groups Spent $3.7 Billion in 2020 to Promote Killing Babies in Abortions Worldwide," Feb. 15, 2022). No need to wonder why Planned Parenthood and their allies are continuing to win the abortion public relations battle.

In 2019, the Virginia GOP held both houses of the legislature. In the election that year, Democrat candidates received 274,000 individual donations of $200 or less, while all Republican candidates received 19,000 individual donations of $200 or less (Virginia Public Access Project, 2019 House and Senate). And of course, the Democrats swept the elections—winning everything. And still the Virginia GOP didn't get the message. In 2020, Joe Biden carried Virginia by 10 points.

These are just a few of many examples to make the point that conservative organization leaders' emphasis on high-dollar donors and ignoring small-dollar donors is doing serious damage to the conservative cause.

Quite frankly, the problem is not at the grassroots level; it's the lack of an entrepreneurial spirit on the part of candidates and those who run conservative organizations. Too many conservative leaders are comfortable running an organization with 5,000, 10,000, or 20,000 mostly high-dollar donors.

As I mentioned in the previous chapter, when the size of a nonprofit organization goes from 10,000 donors to 200,000, the leader's income does not increase 2,000%, but their responsibilities, pressure, stress, and workload go way up.

Grassroots conservatives are worried, frustrated, and angry. They fear for America's future and want and need leadership—but it's in short supply these days.

In 2020, American Target Advertising's (ATA) 70 team members mailed 139 million postal letters for our 17 clients and received about 4.6 million donations from over 1.25 million unique donors. There's no shortage of people who will support conservative causes, but there is a shortage of bold, high-energy, entrepreneurial conservative leadership.

10

Now, Here's Some Good News

In the previous chapters, I've given you lots of scary news and information about how far ahead of conservatives the Left is in grassroots marketing, as well as controlling most all-important institutions and organizations.

However, I remember after Barry Goldwater's landslide loss in 1964 that the political landscape was far more frightening. The conservative movement was in its infancy—just being born.

Things were so bad with a New Deal Democrat, Lyndon Johnson, in the White House, and Democrats with a super majority in the Congress, there were times it almost felt like we were going to be visited with biblical-type plagues—locusts, flies, etc.

The news was so disheartening that I usually waited until the end of the day to read the newspaper, because almost all political news was terrible.

In the 1960s, we had only a few conservative organizations, very few leaders or spokesmen. We had no Fox News TV, Tucker Carlson, Jesse Watters, Mark Levin, Laura Ingraham, etc., or 2,000 conservative talk show hosts, Newsmax, Western Journalism Center, Heritage Foundation, Judicial Watch, etc. But we didn't give up.

After 1964, conservative leaders began to meet and make plans to rise up from the ashes of the Goldwater loss. Bill Buckley Jr. was ready, willing, and able to provide leadership, and he and a small number of others did so. I feel Buckley ran for mayor of New York City in 1965 to help boost our morale.

In October 1964, Ronald Reagan recorded a powerful

speech for Goldwater that was repeated many times on television in the closing weeks of the campaign, but in 1965, he was not seen as a national conservative leader.

Fast forward to 2022 and things again look very dark for conservatives—our liberties hang by a thread. However, even so, today I'm cautiously optimistic for a number of reasons.

First—the Left has made a major miscalculation. For the last 100+ years, they've moved the country to the left relatively cautiously. While their ideas frightened, even terrified, us conservatives, they seldom terrified most voters.

However, all that changed at noon on January 20, 2021, when Democrats took total control of two of our three branches of government. And since then, they've moved hard and far left.

They are now frightening a large majority of Americans. In addition to massive, wasteful spending legislation, which has caused historically high inflation, they are opening the southern borders for all to come, attempting to change our constitutional system of government from three separate co-equal branches of government to just two (by putting the federal courts under the control of a Democrat president and Democrat Senate), and starting a war on police with their "defund the police/soft on crime" tactics that are leading to a huge crime increase.

The Democrats are proposing massive tax increases, moving America quickly from oil and gas to less reliable sun and windmills for power, and teaching our school children through Critical Race Theory that all whites are racists and all minorities are victims. They are also actively promoting sex discussions, including homosexuality and transgenderism with kindergartners.

And they've awakened the voters by quickly moving America toward becoming a socialist/Marxist country. Before January 20, Democrats were moving America left slowly, like a frog in a pot of warm water, but at noon January 20, Democrats quickly started boiling the water, and the American people *en masse* are jumping from the Democrat Party to the Republican Party.

In addition, Democrat President Joe Biden appears frail, incompetent, mentally challenged (reading staff-written notes when speaking "extemporaneously"), and has a vice president who is clearly not up to the job, laughing a strange laugh at inappropriate times, having constant turmoil and turnover in her key staff, and being unable to put words together in a coherent sentence.

The vast majority of Americans agree with us conservatives on most major issues.

Want proof?

Even with most all-elite, powerful, establishment organizations and their leaders actively opposing us, Republicans still have . . .

49% of U.S. House Members
50% of U.S. Senate Members
56% of governors
55% of state legislators

More people self-identify as conservative (36%) than liberal (25%). Moderates make up 37% of the population (*Gallup Poll*, January 2022).

Fox News on average has about 20% more viewers than CNN and MSNBC combined.

Of the 10 most-watched cable news programs in 2021, Fox occupied seven of the 10 slots. The top three were all Fox News shows, with Tucker Carlson ranked number one, drawing in an average of 3.2 million views per night. At number four was MSNBC's Rachel Maddow with 2.5 million views. CNN's most popular TV show, *Anderson Cooper 360*, was ranked number 25 and only had 1.2 million viewers (TVNewser, January 3, 2022).

Since 1987, when the Reagan administration abolished the misnamed "Fairness Doctrine," conservatives have dominated talk radio.

America's largest circulation daily newspaper is the *Wall Street Journal* with 3.5 million print subscribers (Statista.com, Aug. 16, 2021). While the very liberal *New York Times* only has 795,000 print subscribers (NYTimes.com, Nov. 3, 2021).

Hillsdale College's monthly speech digest, *Imprimis*, is mailed to 6.2 million subscribers and has a monthly readership of well over 10 million.

If in the 2022 and 2024 elections over 3 million grassroots conservative volunteers act as modern-day Paul Reveres educating 25, 50, or 100+ of their family, friends, neighbors, church-members, co-workers, high school/college classmates, etc., that *democrats* are responsible for most of America's problems, conservatives will have giant victories.

However, instead of a few men on horseback announcing that the Redcoats or the Regulars are coming (Revere didn't say "the British are coming" because most of your neighbors in Massachusetts in 1775 *were* British), we need 3 million conservatives spreading the word that elite socialist Democrats are coming.

Today conservatives must sound the alarm that the anti-American, anti-police, soft on crime, Critical Race Theory, sexualizing young children, open-borders, elite progressives/socialists/Marxists are coming, and they are all *democrats*.

Because of the new and alternative media, today all of us can be leaders, publishers, journalists, authors, or newscasters. Everyone can be a person of influence by using email, blogging, having a podcast, using Facebook, Twitter, YouTube, and other burgeoning social media, and forwarding videos, emails, e-books, e-pamphlets, white papers, reports, etc., etc.

Some conservatives have blogs or podcasts that reach hundreds or thousands, while others lead or work for nonprofits that have thousands or tens/hundreds of thousands of supporters.

And some conservatives reach millions via websites, talk radio shows, TV shows, appear regularly on radio and TV, and send millions of emails and postal letters.

So, when you combine the activities of all conservatives—from the grandmother who regularly forwards online conservative news articles to 20 family members, to the housewife who daily posts on Facebook to 100 friends, or the pro-life leader whose organization mails tens or hundreds of thousands of postal letters monthly, or the retired senior who forwards conservative material from Heritage Foundation's website, or the Republican state legislator who weekly sends 100,000 emails to his constituents—together we will daily educate over 150 million voters.

Each day this will be 300–400% more than the entire audience of *The New York Times, The Washington Post, TIME Magazine*, ABC, NBC, CBS, CNN, MSNBC, Public TV, and radio combined.

But for the 3 million+ volunteers to be fully engaged in BRANDING the Democrats, they will need 20,000 new conservative organizations and leaders to encourage and train them, supply them with information and material, and educate them in how to be effective.

There's lots of information in this book to help you and your friends start a new conservative organization, grow existing organizations, or run for public office, so what's holding you back? You're the leader America needs.

11

Nationalize the 2022 and 2024
Elections

Republicans never win national elections (presidency, Congress) unless the campaign is fought around conservative issues.

What do I mean by nationalize the elections?

Nationalizing elections means pushing the issues conservatives want the voters to be focused on to the front and center of the campaign. The military leader who selects the place for the battle has a much greater chance of success.

Now is the time for all conservatives to be fully engaged in helping nationalize the 2022 and 2024 elections.

Former Democrat Speaker of the House of Representatives Tip O'Neill famously said, "All politics is local." That's complete nonsense. It's a Democrat strategy to have Republicans focus on Democrat issues and not national issues, which favor Republicans.

The Democrat Party and Democrat politicians are deliverers of services. "If you need a bridge or a road, I'll get right on it. If you need a pothole filled—done. You're not getting your social security check? I'll check on it today. Your schools need money for repairs? I'll take care of it." And on and on and on it goes.

Democrats want conservatives/Republicans to campaign on local issues. A Republican cannot out promise a Democrat when it comes to spending other people's money.

At least 75% of the popular hot button issues that voters feel strongly about are conservative issues.

If you're a Democrat candidate for Congress, which would you rather campaign on: more money for schools, roads, bridges, etc.? Or defend against attacks by a conservative Republican who says you want to raise taxes, open the southern border, relocate illegals in your community (some with criminal records and COVID), teach Critical Race Theory, defund the police, etc.?

Democrat politicians dare not tell the voters their true beliefs, whether they are running for the White House, Congress, governor, city council, school board, etc.

Most of the liberals' victories in recent decades have come from the courts, not the Congress or state legislatures. That's why they fought so hard to keep Justices Neil Gorsuch, Brett Kavanaugh, and Amy Coney Barrett off the Supreme Court.

Remember, I'm not just saying it's important to nationalize the elections, I'm saying they *must* be nationalized around conservative issues. A strong contrast must be drawn between Republican and Democrat views and values, including their worldviews.

If conservatives don't push conservative issues in an election, our enemies, not only Democrat politicians but also Big Media and Big Tech, will censor conservative issues and make the political campaign about the issues that favor Democrats.

Remember the disastrous loss Republicans suffered in 1964 when the Democrats and most of the national media made the Republican candidate Senator Barry Goldwater into a wild and reckless person who was going to cut Social Security benefits and start a world war?

Again, Republicans took heavy losses in 1974 and 1976 because the election was heavily about Watergate.

But when Ronald Reagan framed the 1980 and 1984 presidential elections around conservative issues, including tax cuts, a strong national defense, and traditional values, we scored big victories.

In the 1994 congressional elections, the Republicans took control of Congress for the first time in 40 years. Congressman Newt Gingrich and his team of mostly younger congressmen framed the campaign around a ten-point contract with America with special emphasis on HillaryCare.

And we all remember the Tea Party elections of 2010 and 2014, when Republicans took back Congress with heavy emphasis on ObamaCare.

By the way, if an election is to be nationalized around conservative issues, it will almost certainly need to be done by conservatives. Establishment Republicans are uncomfortable campaigning on conservative issues, especially cultural issues—mostly because they are not conservative; they are Big Government Republicans.

Republican consultants are yelling via emails, postal letters, phone calls, fundraising receptions, breakfasts, lunches, and dinners that all it will take to beat the Democrats in 2022 is more money, i.e., "Send my candidate a lot of money and we'll win."

As I say in Chapter 18, where I quote Morton Blackwell, "Most Republican campaign consultants are content-free."

How will you know if the campaign is nationalized around our issues?

If a campaign is nationalized around conservative issues, not only will the candidate, his campaign team, and his campaign surrogates be stressing the conservative issues, but the issues will be front and center on the TV news shows, talk radio, newspapers, magazines, social media, etc.

And this is a job not just for conservative candidates and national conservatives but all conservatives, whether you operate at the national, state, or local level. All can forward articles to family and friends. If you blog, have a podcast, Tweet, post on YouTube, Facebook, or Snapchat, you're needed to help nationalize the 2022 and 2024 elections.

It's Paul Revere Time, Folks

It's time for each and every conservative to be a modern-day Paul Revere—alerting others about the dangers we face from Democrats.

Don't wait for orders from President Trump, Jesse, Tucker, Hannity, Levin, GOP leaders, or me. Rush to the sound of the battle.

You know what you can do, so please start today. Each of us has different talents and resources available to us—use them.

Most of America's problems are crises because of the policies, programs, and actions of Democrats.

Become a Modern-Day Paul Revere Telling Voters That . . .

- Millions of illegal aliens are flooding into our neighborhoods, towns, and cities through the southern border that the Democrats opened in January 2021. Many are bringing COVID and crime to our communities. Democrats are anxious to have them become citizens and voters (or maybe not even bother with the citizen part).
- Police departments are having their budgets cut, police are retiring early, and morale is at an all-time low because the Democrats focus on defunding the police. Attacks on the character of the police are causing crime to soar, especially murder.
- Big city Democrat prosecutors are refusing to prosecute and/or jail criminals. They are turning hardened career criminals loose into our communities.
- Democrats want to abolish our Constitution and turn America into a one-party elite socialist/Marxist country.

- Democrats want to change election laws, so that only they can win elections. They want to abolish any requirement for voter identification.
- Inflation is out of control because the Democrats are pouring trillions of dollars into the economy to buy votes, which drives up the cost of a finite number of products.
- Democrat educators (unions, school boards, teachers) are sexualizing our young children, including encouraging them to change their biological gender, and teaching all children that if you're white, you're a racist, and minorities are victims of white's domination and racism.

For conservatives to BRAND the Democrats and to have big victories in 2022, 2024, and far beyond we must tie the Democrat Party and Democrat candidates to the crises in America, including all of the issues listed above, plus dozens of others. Remember, if millions of us conservatives do our part, we'll successfully BRAND the Democrats in such a way they never again will be able to win a national election.

12

"It's the Primaries, Stupid"

Some of you will remember James Carville, a Clinton confidant/advisor in the 1992 presidential campaign who famously said, over and over to drive the point home to Democrats, "It's the economy, stupid." Carville wanted Democrats to focus primarily on the weak economy—and it worked. The Republican presidential candidate, George H. W. Bush, a sitting president received only 37.5% of the vote.

I paraphrase Carville and say, *"It's the primaries, stupid!"*

All indications are that there will be a big red wave that crashes onto the political landscape this November 8, 2022, which will sweep out of office many thousands of elected Democrat officials, including some who have previously won by big margins.

About 95% of voters vote straight party tickets. They vote for all Republicans or all Democrats on the ballot, so that when the November red tsunami lands, many "safe" Democrats will go down to defeat.

There are 519,682 political positions in the 50 states that are filled by elections (Poliengine.com), so this November and in future elections there will be hundreds of thousands of opportunities to be running for office.

Therefore, I urge conservatives to contest every position that will be on the ballot. If there isn't anyone opposing the Democrat, seek someone to be a candidate.

If an effective conservative holds the office and is running for re-election, fine. If not, seek someone to be a candidate, because it does the cause of constitutional liberty little good to elect a Congress full of RINOs or a school board full of teachers' union shills.

And if you can't find a strong limited-government constitutional conservative to run, then you must step up, run, and be the leader you are looking for.

You become a leader by getting out of your comfort zone and organizing people to follow your lead.

Again, I say, *"It's the primaries, stupid!"* because it will be a massive loss in our effort to save America if when the November red tsunami wipes out tens of thousands of Democrats their replacements are Big Government establishment Republicans.

Not only is it important that there be a principled constitutional conservative candidate on the ballot in each position, but conservatives need to unite behind the most effective anti-Republican-establishment candidate.

Most all Republican candidates will promise that they are a true red-blooded conservative (whatever that means). However, the truth is most will cave when pressured by Republican leaders to vote to expand government. This is true both at the national and state levels.

Big Government Republican leaders like Kevin McCarthy, Steve Scalise, Mitch McConnell, John Thune, and John Cornyn tell us over and over they are conservative, and it's important to elect more Republicans like them—however, they regularly lie to the voters, especially to us conservatives.

Quite frankly, Pelosi, Schumer, Biden, and all other socialist Democrats have not lied to us. They tell us they are going to massively expand government, do away with traditional moral values, and weaken our national defense, and they are true to their word.

In March 2022, Republican congressional leaders McCarthy, McConnell, and others worked with Democrats to pass a $1.5

trillion budget that grew discretionary spending by 6%, not counting Ukraine and COVID-19 supplemental spending.

Republican congressional leaders even worked to bring back the corrupt practice of "earmarks" for their vote buying projects: $750,000 for a baseball field in Lowell, Massachusetts; $349,000 for swine waste management in North Carolina, etc. (DailyWire.com, March 9, 2022).

The spending bill also included $575 million for "family planning" internationally; $286 million for Title X funding to "keep the lights on at Planned Parenthood"; $32.5 million for the pro-abortion UN Population Fund; and $200 million for a brand new "Gender, Equity, and Equality Action Fund" to help promote abortion across the globe. Additionally, $523 million is going to the UN Global Health Programs, some of which will fund abortions (DailyWire.com, March 9, 2022).

By the way, another important advantage of running a candidate for every position on the ballot is that it will increase the vote for every other Republican candidate. Each candidate on the ballot has family, friends, neighbors, fellow church members, etc., who will cast their vote for their friend who otherwise would not have voted. And when voting for their Republican friend will probably vote for all other Republican candidates.

Also, if the campaign is not successful, the cause is still advanced. New people will be registered to vote, educated, and activated for the conservative cause, etc. Also, incumbents who previously ignored you and your issues will likely be more responsive. As the saying goes, "You're guaranteed to lose if you don't try."

As I survey the 2022 political landscape, I am reminded that in 1977 and 1978 my late friend the great Howard Phillips visited every congressional district in America. During a trip to New Hampshire in 1977, only five people showed up for a meeting. One of them was an Allegheny Airlines copilot named Gordon Humphrey, who volunteered to run against Democrat Thomas J. McIntyre. Gordon became one of three new New Right U.S. Senators elected in 1978. He ran when few thought he could win.

Howard Phillips, Gordon Humphrey, and the rest of us in the New Right of that era understood the lesson of Babe Ruth's 1927 season. That year the Bambino led the major leagues with 60 home runs, but he also led in strikeouts with 89. We weren't worried about how the establishment, the press, and others would view us if we lost. We knew if you expected to hit a lot of home runs you had to swing at a lot of pitches and expect to strike out a lot.

For more than a hundred years, we conservatives have had our political guns trained on the wrong target. We've been focused primarily on defeating the liberal, Big Government Democrats, when the first, and most important, roadblock to our goal of governing America according to conservative principles is the Big Government Republicans.

During the entire centuries-long civil war in the Republican Party, the progressive establishment leadership of the GOP has been selling the notion that the Democrats and the liberals are the problem, and that if conservatives would only line up behind establishment Republicans and put them in charge of the federal government, the growth of government and America's slide toward socialism would stop.

Nothing could be further from the truth.

Establishment Republicans are not conservative. Establishment Republicans do not offer a coherent conservative worldview as an alternative to the Democrats' secular liberal worldview; they pursue policies that are "Democrat-lite," and they govern as "dime-store Democrats" (Barry Goldwater's term to describe President Eisenhower's policies), simply growing government at a slightly slower pace. Consequently, the abusive bureaucracies and extra-constitutional rules and regulations, which establishment Republicans either support or to which they offer little or no opposition, have continued to grow.

Moreover, the GOP establishment has been complicit in one of the worst abuses Washington's insiders have perpetrated on America's taxpayers—the Democrats' decades-long programs have wasted trillions of taxpayer dollars on slush funds for leftwing causes such as NPR, Public TV, Legal Services Corp., Planned Parenthood, radical environmentalism, homosexual and ethnic advocacy groups such as La Raza, and the various ACORN clones of the Left that so offend conservatives and are committed to defeating Republicans and advancing a far-left agenda.

Far from shrinking government, whenever they have been in power, establishment Republicans have contributed to the growth of government. The GOP leadership can't hide behind the excuse that Republicans don't have the presidency or a congressional majority, because when Republicans have the White House, House of Representatives, *and* Senate, funding for Planned Parenthood and other liberal causes still increase.

Merely having an R next to your name on the ballot does not mean you will hold fast to limited-government constitutional conservative principles. As I documented in my book, *Conservatives Betrayed*, the time that President George W. Bush occupied the White House and the Republican establishment led a Republican majority in Congress certainly demonstrates such a claim is false.

How do conservatives get to Washington? How do conservatives govern America?

It's the primaries, stupid!

In the 1950s and 1960s, the conservative movement was a coalition built around two issues: economic conservatism and anti-communist national defense conservatism. This gave us a base to occasionally win an election but was not enough to build a successful national governing majority.

That all changed in the latter part of the 1970s when social conservatives added their strength to the movement and Ronald Reagan came forward as the standard-bearer for conservative ideas.

Republicans won three landslide presidential elections in the 1980s, but we were still only slowing the erosion of our freedoms because we were still burdened by the deadwood of the business-as-usual wing of the Republican Party, and its addiction to "Democrat-lite" policy and spending.

For over 50 years I have been saying that to change things and stop the slide to socialism, two things needed to happen: first, things need to get really bad really fast; and second, there needs to be some political vehicle, some means for the people to channel their anger, and to translate their outrage into political action.

Guess what: we're there.

Once, twice, three times a day, Democrats are going to do something to make you angry—that's okay. Take 30 or 40 seconds, maximum, to let off some steam, and then get down on your knees and thank the good Lord for the excesses of Biden, Schumer in the Senate, and Nancy Pelosi as Speaker of the House.

Because of the failures, crises, and disasters caused by Democrats, conservatives have the opportunity of a century—no guarantee, just the opportunity—to end the erosion of our liberties and return us to the constitutional principles our Founders envisioned.

Conservative activists, parents, grandparents, independents—unfettered by old ties and old relationships with Washington's Republican establishment—have brought a new willingness to engage in the primary election battles necessary to prune away the dead wood of the Republican establishment and make way for the growth of a new Republican Party committed to pro-American, limited-government constitutional conservatism.

Their influence in Republican primaries will ensure that voters have a stark choice between Big Government Republicans, who have been complicit in the Democrats' decades-long campaign to recast America into a collective-centered society built around an intrusive central government, and limited-government constitutional conservative candidates who stand for American exceptionalism based on individualism, liberty, and the sanctity of the human spirit.

The turnaround we've been working for isn't going to happen with one election. We will have much work to do to find and support candidates who are prepared to fend off the inevitable calls to return to old ways of compromise instead of standing on principles. As we enter the 2022 and 2024 election cycles, I'm more optimistic about the future of this great country than I've ever been, because liberty-loving voters, including parents and forgotten Americans, are finally beginning to understand—*It's the primaries, stupid!*

Strategy for the Primaries

If you are involved in politics in your precinct, town, or county, gather at your home or some convenient location with other limited-government constitutional conservatives to develop a vision, goals, strategy, and tactics/projects plan. If you are a state leader of a conservative organization, bring together your peers to do the same.

Here Are 10 Key Qualities to Look For in a Candidate

1. Is committed to building the conservative movement.
2. A boat rocker.
3. Walks with conservatives, not with establishment Republicans.
4. Well-read on conservative philosophy.

13

The State of the Conservative Movement and What's Needed to Win and Govern America

In 1955, William F. Buckley Jr. wrote, in the first edition of *National Review*, "It [*National Review*] stands athwart history yelling, 'Stop . . . .'"

Thus, today's conservative movement was born.

In September 1960, Young Americans for Freedom (YAF) was founded on Bill Buckley Jr.'s family estate in Sharon, Connecticut.

In August 1961, I left Houston and went to New York City to lead YAF as executive secretary, and a year later I began a major study of direct mail/marketing, which continues to this day.

In 1964, conservatives nominated Barry Goldwater for president, and in November he lost in a landslide—39% to LBJ's 61%. Goldwater received 27,178,188 votes. In 2020, President Trump received 74,222,958 votes. This, in many respects, is a measure of how the conservative movement has grown and succeeded, even for those who do not consider Donald Trump a movement conservative (and he is not).

In the summer of 1964, I hired six women to copy by hand the names of 12,500 Goldwater $50+ donors from the public records in the clerk of the U.S. House of Representatives. This small list allowed me in January 1965 to start the world's first political/ideological direct mail/direct marketing agency with one client—YAF.

In the 1960s, I began to pioneer the use of direct mail to raise money, pass or defeat legislation, elect and defeat candidates, educate and activate voters, and to enlist millions of new people into the conservative movement.

There would not be a conservative movement worthy of being called a movement without direct mail. The Post Office is a government agency that has greatly benefited conservatives.

In my opinion, Ronald Reagan would not have gotten 49% of the Republican Convention delegates in 1976, nor become the GOP candidate for president in 1980, without direct mail.

Under the leadership of his longtime aide, Lyn Nofziger, Reagan acquired 250,000 (mostly $5, $10, $15, $25, $50) donors in both the 1976 and 1980 campaigns. While his competitors (Ford, Bush, Dole, Baker, and Connelly) were funding their campaign with thousands of $500 and $1,000 donations, Reagan's campaign was fueled by hundreds of thousands of small donations.

Also, Reagan's campaign was supported by hundreds of national, state, and local conservative organizations that were launched in the 1960s and 1970s and sustained by millions of low-dollar direct mail donors.

In the 1970s and 1980s, dozens of national conservative organizations had 100,000, 200,000, 300,000+ donors/supporters/subscribers, including Senator Jesse Helms's National Congressional Club, the American Conservative Union, Phyllis Schlafly's Eagle Forum, the *National Review*, my monthly magazine *Conservative Digest*, National Conservative Political Action Committee (NCPAC), Gun Owners of America, Jerry Falwell's Moral Majority, Americans United for Life, American Security Council, Christian Coalition, Young Americans for Freedom, National Right to Work Foundation, The Conservative Caucus, National Tax Limitation Committee, Pat Robertson's 700 Club, etc., etc.

Most of these organizations are no longer active or they are a fraction of their former size, and few new ones have taken their place. Conservatives dominated grassroots marketing in the 1960s–80s; however, today the Left is far, far ahead.

How far?

As I've previously written, for at least the last 20 years, liberals have raised about 700% more money from about 700% more donors from their nonprofit organizations. I estimate the Left has about 21 million+ donors that yearly contribute about $21 billion. In that same period of time, conservatives yearly raise about $3–4 billion from 3–4 million donors.

Of course, conservatives have some leaders with high energy and entrepreneurial spirits who lead large, impactful organizations, such as Dr. Ed Feulner who, with the late and great John Von Kannon, built the Heritage Foundation into the world's largest think tank; Dr. Larry Arnn, president of Hillsdale College; Tom Fitton, president of Judicial Watch; Dr. Ralph Reed's Faith and Freedom Coalition; Reverend Pat Robertson, 700 Club; Alan Sears and (since 2017) Michael Farris, presidents and CEOs of Alliance Defending Freedom; Farris also founded Patrick Henry College and Home School Legal Defense Association; Wayne LaPierre, president of the NRA; and of course the person I dedicated *GO BIG* to, Morton Blackwell, president and founder of the Leadership Institute; as well as a few others, but not nearly as many as the Left has.

Also, I'm concerned that many conservatives think there will be a red tsunami wave that will wash Democrats out of office in November 2022, so they believe they don't have to do anything. Because victory is close, all we have to do is keep doing what we've been doing the last 30 years, and we will have a big victory in November 2022. America's future will be secure. Morton Blackwell called this strain of thought "succumbing to the Sir Galahad Theory of politics—we will win because we are self-evidently right."

What do conservatives need to govern America?

Conservatives Need:

- **20,000+ new national, state, and local single-issue organizations**. The Left has over 20,000 vs. about 1,000–2,000 for conservatives.
- **20 million grassroots donors** regularly supporting conservative organizations. Conservatives now have 3–4 million, while the Left has 21 million+.
- **Dozens of mega donors** investing billions of dollars into the conservative movement. The Left has many George Soros, Bill Gates, Jeff Bezos, Michael Bloomberg, Tom Steyer, and Mark Zuckerberg-types.
- **Thousands of high-level professional direct marketers.**
- **Thousands of high-level professional development people** to raise high-dollar donations. Most every national conservative organization either does not have a development department or is understaffed.
- **Thousands of new high-energy, young (under 40) conservatives** to become leaders of nonprofits.
- **Thousands of boat-rocking, principled conservative candidates to run in primaries** challenging silent, ineffective, establishment Republicans for Congress, state, and local offices.
- **Thousands of new, single-issue internet news sites** that will communicate the truth to 100 million+ Americans.
- **Hundreds and hundreds of for-profit businesses** that will help conservative leaders, candidates, and organizations market themselves, raise small-dollar donations, raise major gifts, acquire legacy bequests, win elections, advise on media matters, consult on business issues, legal issues, etc. Ben Franklin said,

"There's no accounting for the amount of good a person can accomplish if they make a business out of it."

In order to make major changes in America, it's necessary to build a big grassroots movement around a moral or ethical cause and preferably led by a strong, articulate, charismatic leader.

Since 1950, there have been a number of issues that have become national causes leading to major changes in America's culture, laws, and politics, including the sexual revolution, safe cars, safe driving, the environment, civil rights, progressivism, anti-communism, the conservative movement, and the Tea Party movement.

In recent years, the Left has abandoned many important positions and issues they previously supported, including free speech, religious freedom, safety/law-and-order/police, blue collar workers, and traditional moral values.

Now for conservatives/Republicans, there's a new cause that has the potential to be far more powerful than recent conservative causes, because it's caught the attention of a massive group: *parents.*

The Parents Revolt
The war that the progressive liberal Democrats are engaged in against parents and school children is shocking. It's likely to do massive harm to the future of the Democrat party.

The most public issue in the new parents' movement is the teaching of Critical Race Theory (CRT). The essence of the message is that America's very founding was racist, and it is fundamentally still a racist country. All whites are racist, and all non-whites are victims is what the Democrats are teaching our children.

However, there are many other issues driving the parents' revolution, including:

- Democrats insist that boys who feel like they are girls should be allowed to compete in girls' sports and use girls' bathrooms and showers.
- Democrat school officials and teachers are urging children as young as five and six years old to consider changing their biological sex, and Democrat educators are telling them they can have sex-changing surgery and medicine without their parents' knowledge.
- Democrats have identified 55 new/different genders children are allowed to call themselves in addition to boys and girls.
- Democrats don't want parents involved in their children's schools. Remember, former Virginia Governor and Chairman of the Democratic National Committee Terry McAuliffe, in a September 2021 debate with the now Republican Governor of Virginia Glenn Youngkin, said, "I don't think parents should be telling schools what they should teach."

14

Internet Marketing

Direct mail is a mature form of advertising/marketing.

Not so, the internet.

We'll figure out how to market on the internet. It might happen in a year or two, but more likely in 5–10+ years.

Over the last 100+ years the giants who came before us in direct mail/marketing not only conducted and practiced world-class direct mail/marketing, but they left roadmaps and instructions for us in the form of thousands of articles and books.

Some of my personal favorites are my two direct mail mentors, Ed Mayer Jr. and Dick Benson, as well as Rosser Reeves, John Caples, Pete Hoke, Bob Stone, Bill Jayme, and Brian Kurtz.

Often when a new technology is developed, it has quick growth but since people haven't figured out how to monetize it—it comes crashing down, and over the coming years it's rebuilt slowly as people figure out a business model.

This happened with railroads in the first half of the 1800s and for automobiles in the early 1900s.

Radio became popular in the early 1920s, but not profitably, which limited their usage until the mid-1920s. The business model that was developed was that radio stations gave away the content and charged businesses to advertise.

This also happened with the internet. It took off like a skyrocket in the mid-1990s and came crashing down to earth in 1999 and 2000.

Of course, lots of money has been made with the internet, but it's mostly those who supply the services, including hardware and software.

It's similar to a gold strike. Most of the money is made by those who sell the food, picks, shovels, blue jeans, run the dance halls, saloons, etc.

Today (2022), most internet political fundraising seems to be done by amateurs, likely people in their twenties who have never studied marketing and likely never read a marketing book.

Because the cost to send a political fundraising email is so inexpensive, it allows people who literally know nothing about fundraising to try it.

The cost to send a political fundraising email is about .001¢ per email. However, the cost to mail a postal political fundraising letter before COVID was about 60¢, but post-COVID the cost is around 75¢ or more if you use nonprofit postage. If you mail using bulk rate or first-class postage, the cost is closer to $1.00 per letter.

Obviously, the professional skills required to spend $100 for 100,000 emails vs. $75,000 for 100,000 postal letters is very different; however, the long-term benefits of acquiring thousands of postal donors from the 100,000 list is far greater than getting a handful of small donors from the email.

A Digital Marketing Checklist

- About one third of the people will go to the internet to check you out before making a decision as to whether or not to send a donation.
- Make sure that your website reinforces your fundraising. If you write to people saying you have a crisis and need money quickly and they go to your website and see no mention of it, there's an obvious disconnect.
- Don't let a techy/software professional design your website. They build the website, but the design and content should be done by someone who has marketing skills.

- Use multi-marketing channels when available. If you have a postal address and an email address, send the postal mailing, then follow up with an email, and the results will be greater than just using one channel. Also, if you have a phone number, call using robo-calls and tell them to be on the lookout for a letter/email.
- The most important line in your address is not the subject line—it's the FROM line. Think about how you evaluate emails. If they're from a family member or a friend, it doesn't matter what the subject line is—because of who it's from you're going to open it.
- A high percentage of those whose first contribution is via the internet will not send a second contribution digitally. Therefore, make a significant effort to get their postal address for future solicitations.
- Each technology that can be used for mass communication has some unique quality about it. For example, the unique quality of the radio is the sound of the human voice, for TV it's moving pictures (baseball used to be America's number one pastime, now it's football—better pictures). And if you don't understand what the unique quality of the internet is, you won't maximize your opportunities.

What's unique about the internet is that it's interactive. You don't interact with a book, newspaper, radio, or TV. Most political/ideological websites are used like a brochure. They put up a lot of boring, uninteresting material and pictures, and once someone has seen it there's not any reason for them to return to the site. You may not like your daily newspaper, but you still pay them money each day to get the day's newspaper because it's different each day. Make your website interactive—post letters, have petitions, surveys, contests.

Give someone in the campaign "ownership" of daily updating your website.

15

Viguerie's DOs and DON'Ts
of Marketing

Before setting out to raise money via postal mail, digital/email, phones, or in-person, review this list. Follow my advice and you'll raise significantly more money.

Because I'm covering many issues in *GO BIG* and trying to solve many problems conservative nonprofits face, I'll repeat advice in multiple chapters.

When I do repeat, it's not a mistake—it's because I think it's really important to comprehend, understand, and remember what I'm saying. It's often said that the number one "secret" of advertising is repetition.

You may have heard the story about a preacher who gave powerful and impactful sermons. When asked why he thought his sermons were so effective he replied,

> *"Well, I tells them what I'm going to tell them.*
> *Then I tells them.*
> *Then I tells them what I told them."*

The DOs

1. **Four Horsemen:** Be sure you have a written Four Horsemen of Marketing for your organization. Pay special attention to POSITION (your niche in the market-place). How are you different from others? If you're not different from others, why support you? See Chapter 2.

2. **Brand:** It's exceedingly difficult to raise lots of money without a strong BRAND. And you as an individual should also have a BRAND. See Chapter 3.

3. **Tagline:** Anything written for your organization or candidate needs to have a tagline. The tagline should allow someone to grasp within a few seconds what separates your organization, your cause, or your candidate from all others. See Chapter 4.

4. **Four-Part Plan:** Have you written a Newt Four-Part Plan? Remember, the main benefit to writing a plan is **Writing the Plan**—it helps to clarify and crystalize your thoughts. The plan should include who's in charge of the project, a start and finish date, budget, etc. See Chapter 6.

5. **Do You Have a Project?** Have one or more specific projects focused on solving a particular problem, such as you need $8,500 to produce a video that says Democrats want to defund the police. Or you need $40,000 to run the video on Facebook for two weeks to reach 500,000 single women and seniors before election day.

6. **Start Letters with a Technique:** Start all acquisition letters and most mailings to previous donors with a marketing technique, such as a survey, poll, petition, or a coin or real dollar bill attached to the first page, a negotiable check for $1 or $2 dollars, a pseudo check for a larger amount (e.g., $20.22), a bumper sticker or two, a booklet, etc. A mailing with multiple techniques will usually raise more money than with one technique, and one technique crushes no technique.

7. **Big Vision:** Present a big vision. If you want to raise big dollars, you need a big vision. "Where there is no vision, the people perish" —Proverbs 29:18 (KJV).

8. **Project Urgency, Courage, Energy:** Project a sense of urgency, courage, and energy. Conservatives know we're in bad shape and can lose our country soon. Of all the things conservatives want or need, perhaps, number one is strong, bold, aggressive leaders. Think Donald Trump, Ron DeSantis, Ted Cruz, Jim Jordan, Elon Musk, and Mark Levin.

9. **Put Donors First:** Remember, it's about the donor and *their* interest—whether you're asking for money face-to-face, on the phone, via letters (house, acquisition, thank you notes, newsletters), online, etc.

    It's not about you and/or your organization. It's about issues and your ideas/projects for solutions to problems that concern the potential donor.

10. **When Possible, Establish a Monthly Giving Program:** One of the best books on starting and operating a monthly giving program is *Monthly Giving Made Easy* by Erica Waasdorp.

11. **Publish Newsletters:** Publish (print and/or digital) a regular newsletter that reports on your activities. For help with your newsletter, I strongly recommend Tom Ahern's book, *Making Money with Donor Newsletters.*

12. **Seek Out One or More Mentors:** None of us are turtles on a stump. If you see a turtle on a stump, you know it didn't get there by itself. Someone picked it up and put it there. Look for mentors in your personal and professional life. I did and it made all the difference.

13. **A Development Team Is a Must:** Do have a development team/department if you want to raise lots of money. The primary fundraising benefit of acquiring donors via postal mail and/or digital is to get more and larger gifts in the future from personal contact. See Chapter 19, number 1.

14. **Know The Lifetime Value of Your Donors:** Do estimate the lifetime value (LTV) of a donor. In the early years of a new organization, spend most of your money on acquiring new donors. Your investment in building your donor list should be recovered in 6–12 months. As a general rule, your effectiveness will be determined by the size of your army, including donors, subscribers, members, activists, and volunteers. See Chapter 19, number 4.

15. **Postal Letters:** When writing a postal letter, remember:

   a.   Write the letter to one friend. Then the 10,000+/- letters you send will read more friendly and personal.

   b.   If appropriate, recognize early in the communication your relationship, such as a previous donation, signed a petition, responded to a survey or a poll, shared a position on an issue, etc.

   c.   Include a P.S. that summarizes the main points of your letter. Often the P.S. is one of the first things a person reads in a letter. So, put as much information as possible in a 35–50+ word P.S.

   d.   Keep words, sentences, and paragraphs short. Make sure you have good headlines, underline certain words, make your letter scannable. Most people don't read an entire letter—but they do scan it.

   e.   Include a sheet of paper that's called a "Contribution form." It should restate the purpose of your organization, the project you're raising money for and suggested dollar amounts, who to make the check payable to, and how to make an online contribution; if you have a technique, such as a survey or petition, make reference to it.

f. Enclose an envelope for the donor to use when returning a contribution, survey, petition, etc.

g. If it's appropriate, state a need for urgency. Doing so will increase returns.

h. Does your website support/reinforce your fund-raising? Keep your website current and refer people to it. Remember, about one third of the people will check you out online before making a contribution.

i. As a general rule, the more you tell, the more you raise. Don't be afraid of long letters, and don't listen to anyone who tells you, "Keep your letters short. I don't read long letters." A good eight-page letter will out-perform a good seven-page letter and a good four-page letter will out-perform a good three-page letter, etc.

j. Invest in growth. Yes, I know you want to build a large list of donors and make lots of net dollars all at the same time. Be sure you're sitting down when you read the next sentence: It's not going to happen (short-term)—not today, not tomorrow, not ever. You have to be willing to invest money to make lots of money (long-term). If you're not willing to invest lots of money to build a big organization, you'll never have a big organization.

k. If you're only asking your donors two, three, or four times a year for a donation, you're leaving a lot of money on the table. At ATA we mail for our clients a fundraising mailing about once a month to their donors, and in addition we mail a newsletter once a month with a "soft ask" for money. If you're raising money for a political candidate or committee, you can mail much more frequently in the closing months of the campaign.

   l. When sending a postal mailing to your donors, if you also have their email address, send the postal mailing to them as an email.

   m. Always stay inside your BRAND. If you don't, you will weaken your BRAND and reduce your income.

The DON'Ts

1. **Don't Parachute into Your Donor's Life:** If they are a previous donor, don't parachute into their lives. In other words, write as you would to a friend—you're having an ongoing conversation. Make reference to previous communication, correspondence, and requests, including results and outcomes of previous requests. Of course, be sure to acknowledge any previous support and the good it achieved.

2. **Don't Think of Donors as ATMs:** When communicating with a donor, inquire as to what are their main concerns, frustrations, issues, and perhaps you can offer an idea as to how your organization can help deal with their concerns. Avoid conversations that treat them as if they are an ATM.

3. **Don't Forget that the Best 20% of Your Donors Will Contribute 80% of Your Money.**

4. **Don't Forget to Ask for a Donation:** It's an old saying, but very, very true: "The number one reason a person gives a donation is—because they are asked."

5. **Don't Put a Low-Energy Person in a Key Position That Requires High Energy:** You'll be disappointed at their lack of progress, and they'll be frustrated and discouraged. Low-energy people have a role to play, but not in a key, high impactful position. High-energy people make things happen.

    A bright, high-energy person can and will learn

particular skills, but it's almost impossible to turn a low-energy person into someone with high energy.

6. **Don't Ignore Small Donations:** Small donations like $5, $10, $15, etc., come from your foot soldiers, your army. In war you need artillery, tanks, ships, and airplanes, which you may think of as your large donors. But if you don't have foot soldiers, you won't win long term.

16

What You Can Do to Save America

I'm regularly asked by friends, acquaintances, and strangers, *"What can I do to save America?"*

This usually follows a speech by me or a conversation about the threat to America from the progressives/Marxists.

There can be no compromise with today's Democrats because what is at stake is the future of Constitutional Liberty. With Democrats in control of Congress and the White House, the political debate is no longer about how many employees the Department of Agriculture should have or whether to spend money on Defense or Welfare. The New Democrats have made it clear they hate the America that you and I love and intend to fundamentally remake our government and its traditional powers.

We Are in a Spiritual Civil War

In a very real sense, the New Democrats have declared war on the Constitution as it has been understood for 245 years and on those who love America and hold traditional moral values, as well as conservative beliefs about the liberties protected by the Bill of Rights.

If we are to save our Constitutional Republic, it will only be done by Americans at the grassroots level getting involved in a way they never have because the vast majority of people/voters get most all of their political information from Democrats.

Big Media (most newspapers, news magazines, network TV, and radio) and Big Tech (including Google, Facebook, YouTube, etc.) are all led by Democrats. In sports terms, the referees have left the sidelines and joined the Democrat team.

Indeed, Big Tech and Big Media executives/owners have become some of the Democrat party's star players, leading the charge to censor and de-platform conservatives, and take away our rights to have a job, to communicate with our friends and family, to buy the products we want to buy, and otherwise live twenty-first century American life in all its richness.

However, as bleak as that reads, we are not without resources, including the fact that the vast majority of Americans agree with conservatives on most important issues, such as:

America Agrees with Conservatives On . . .

- Not packing the Supreme Court
- Securing our southern border, and finish building the wall
- Not making D.C. and Puerto Rico states
- Opposing the "defund the police" movement
- Stopping progressives/Marxists from burning our cities
- Opposing tax hikes
- Opposing teaching CRT in schools
- No sexualizing of school children
- Requiring identification to vote
- Etc., etc.

YOU Are the Answer

In the 2020 presidential campaign, issues that would be a negative for Joe Biden and the Democrats were censored by network TV, newspapers, and Big Tech, including the Hunter Biden scandal; Biden's mental and physical status; and Democrats' pledge to raise taxes, loosen border control, provide unlimited taxpayer-funded abortions, etc.

Since Big Media, Big Tech, and all other major American institutions are opposed to us and are deliberately preventing

Americans from getting accurate information—who does that leave? The answer is—*you.*

Yes, *you,* and millions of grassroots Americans (young, middle-aged, seniors, students, working, retired) can do and, in fact, must do all we can to educate our immediate families, as well as our extended families (aunts, uncles, cousins), our friends, neighbors, fellow church members, co-workers, old school friends, etc., etc.

What we are lacking is leadership.

The fact is, we are the leaders we have been looking and waiting for.

There are many, many things that each of us can do to help save our wonderful country, but this can't be something we only think about when Election Day is on the horizon. If we are to succeed, each of us must make saving America part of our daily routine.

Here's my list. Perhaps you can think of other ways. If so, email me at rav@gobigconservatives.com.

Action Items to Save America

1.   Check-in regularly at conservativehq.org and feduppac.org. We focus on providing ideas and information about what conservatives need to do to advance the conservative cause. In other words, we don't take up your time cussing out the liberals. As a conservative activist, you know progressives/Marxists are mean, evil, and dangerous. What you need is information, ideas, material, articles, videos, and books to share with others.

2.   Build an e-list and forward good information to family, friends, etc.

3.   Build a big Twitter following and tweet or re-tweet something most every day. Keep an eye on your Parler

and other social media accounts and do the same.

4. Start a blog. You can start small with family and friends. FedUpPAC.org and ConservativeHQ.org will have lots of material you can use for ideas. Most of the material is not copyrighted, so you can use it as you like.

5. The Left has over 20,000 single-issue national, state, and local nonprofit organizations. Conservatives have about 1,000–2,000. Call family/friends and start an organization based on your interests, such as the Second Amendment, local public-school issues, support for the local police, ballot security, border security, etc.

   Every organization, committee, and task force needs a president, vice president, secretary/treasurer, membership chairman, media director, event planner, fundraiser, etc. Get people involved and give them a title. From this expanded leadership pool, the cream will rise to the top and we'll have future candidates for school board, city council, state legislature, Congress, etc.

6. If you don't want to help lead a group, encourage others to do so and support them with a donation.

7. Donate to national, state, and local nonprofits and politicians whose views, values, and activities you're in agreement with.

8. Become knowledgeable and articulate on public policy issues by listening/watching conservative hosts on FOX, Newsmax, OneAmerica, Sinclair, radio and TV including Jesse Watters, Tucker Carlson, Laura Ingraham, Mark Levin, Ben Shapiro, and Dennis Prager.

9. Get involved in your local Republican party, perhaps first at a precinct or county level. If your precinct doesn't have a chairman—volunteer to be the

chairman. Also, volunteer to serve on committees and task forces. Go to the meetings and become a delegate to the county, state, and national conventions.

10. Don't give the enemy support in any way, including money. Years ago, I stopped buying *The New York Times*, *The Washington Post*, and watching NBC, CBS, ABC, etc. Patronize your local, independent (and most likely conservative) small-business men and women.

11. Encourage and support conservative media, publications, books, websites. To help you find these sources, we quote and link to them regularly on ConservativeHQ.org and FedUpPAC.org.

12. Volunteer and help political candidates at the local, state, and national levels.

13. Sign-up to work at the polls on Election Day. If you can't do that, volunteer to work whatever hours you can outside the voting area.

14. Talk to family, friends, neighbors—but especially to your young children and grandchildren. In the mid-1970s, I was out west with my 12-year-old daughter, Renée. Some friends (a husband and wife who were national conservative leaders) invited us to dinner. At dinner was a "prodigal son" who had, at college, wandered away from his parents' views and values, but had returned.

I asked my friends at the dinner table, "When he was a boy, did you talk to him about your views and values?" and they said, "No." Please don't make that mistake. By example and words, share your views, values, and politics with your children, grandchildren, nieces, nephews, etc.

15. Give gift subscriptions to publications that will educate and reinforce your views, values, and politics. I subscribe to the *Wall Street Journal*, *Epoch Times*, and

Imprimis for my daughters, Renée and Michelle, and my grandchildren.

16. Write, call, and meet with elected officials, including members of Congress and state legislatures—especially Democrats. They need to hear from you.

17. Encourage, urge, and push family, friends, neighbors, and others who share your politics to be registered and to vote.

18. Let others know how you feel. Liberals are quick to often and loudly share with one and all their views and values. Conservatives also need to share with others your vision and values. Get lots of bumper stickers that support your political views; put one or two on your car and give the others to those who share your views.

19. Subscribe to Hillsdale College's free *Imprimis* newsletter, take Hillsdale's free online classes, and study and arm yourself with the knowledge necessary to promote and defend the conservative position around the dinner table, with co-workers, online, and in your everyday conversations.

20. Go to FEDUPPAC.org and forward this chapter or the entire book (it's free online) and other conservative material to family, friends, neighbors, and others. This is how we're going to get tens of millions of new people educated and involved in saving America.

Conservatives as Modern-day Paul Reveres Can Save America

Folks, there is a *spiritual civil war* going on in America. Progressives/Marxists are committed to driving God, traditional values, and conservatives out of America. The only thing standing between them and success is us—conservative grassroots Americans.

The bottom line is, we're going to save America by educating and empowering millions of grassroots Americans like YOU to become modern-day Paul Reveres, spreading the word to family, friends, neighbors, and others that the socialists/Marxists are in control of the federal government.

Educating and encouraging others to join us will be like a spring of water bubbling up from the ground, or raindrops that fall to the ground and become a small stream. The small streams one by one begin to join together and become a small creek, and as the creek grows, it becomes a small river. Many small rivers will join together and as millions of conservative efforts come together, you will help build a mighty river that will wash over the progressives lies and anti-American policies.

Lead or Follow, But Please Get Involved Today

I am reminded that on April 19, 1775, at the Battle of Lexington and Concord, no general commanded our patriot ancestors to defend their community and their rights against the British. Those who fought that day simply rushed to the sound of the guns. Today, while our tools are not the muskets of our ancestors—but rather our voices, phones, email, talk radio, blogs, cable TV, websites, and social media—the urgency for individual action is equally pressing.

> "I know thy works, that thou are neither cold nor hot: I would thou wert cold or hot. So then because thou art lukewarm, and neither cold nor hot, I will spue thee out of my mouth."
>
> —Revelation 3:15–16 (KJV)

Don't wait for a conservative leader or a politician to suggest activity. You know there is a war going on between the forces of good and evil. Lead or follow, but please get involved today.

> "Then I heard the voice of the Lord say, 'Whom shall I send? And who will go for us?' and I said, 'Here am I. Send me!'"
>
> —Isaiah 6:8 (KJV)

17

Some Firsthand Stories of How Conservatives Used Direct Mail to Build the Conservative Movement—And Win

As I've said elsewhere in *GO BIG*, there would be no conservative movement worthy of being called a movement without direct mail.

If the Left had ever been able to deny conservatives the use of the Post Office, there probably would not have been a President Ronald Reagan or a Newt Gingrich-led takeover of the U.S. Congress in 1994. The ERA, Common-Situs Picketing legislation, and HillaryCare would have passed into law and most conservative nonprofits would not exist. Also, the GOP would not be competitive financially with the Democrats.

I've recorded a few stories here, mostly lost to history, to remind conservatives of the importance of direct mail, not just to our past but to our future as well. Because with the Leftists' almost total control of the mainstream media and digital platforms that consistently cancel conservative speech and candidates, direct mail/direct marketing holds the key to our ability to be competitive.

1. YAF—First Conservative Nonprofit to Do Large-Scale Direct Mail

I became Young Americans for Freedom's executive secretary in September 1961, and by 1962 I was beginning to aggressively build a large list of donors to YAF.

In the spring of 1962, I wrote to a movie star and asked if he would sign a letter for YAF. Several months later, I received the first page of my letter back. It had been marked up with crayons and in the lower lefthand corner was this message,

Mr. Viguerie, I'm so sorry I just found your letter in Ronnie's toy chest. If you feel my name would be of help to YAF, feel free to use it. —Ronald Reagan

I had developed two types of letters. One focused on the work YAF was doing on college campuses, combatting liberal students and professors. The other letter focused on YAF's political activities, especially encouraging Barry Goldwater to run for president.

It didn't take me long to discover that one of the packages was getting a very good response, and the other not so much.

It was an important lesson I learned early and never forgot. Donors liked the work the young people in YAF were doing to fight young liberals. After all, that was completely in their wheelhouse.

However, when we wrote asking for help to elect conservatives to public office, the response was dismal, and that is as it should be. What do 19, 20, and 21-year-old kids know about defeating Democrat candidates for the U.S. House, U.S. Senate, and the presidency?

By 1964, YAF had over 50,000 donors, and I thought I knew everything there ever was to know about direct mail fundraising. The reality is I did not know 1% of what I now know.

Today, under the longtime leadership of Ron Robinson, YAF is a major conservative organization and a marketing powerhouse to donors, students, and the public. Ron has recently passed the presidency of YAF on to former governor of Wisconsin Scott Walker.

2. H. L. (Bill) Richardson and the Launching of Gun Owners of America

I started my direct mail agency in January 1965, and in March a California friend, Ted Loeffler, asked me to raise money for H. L. (Bill) Richardson, a conservative running in a special election for a state senate seat close to Sacramento.

Using the 12,500 Goldwater $50+ donors list I had acquired from the clerk of the U.S. House of Representatives the previous year, we raised about $70,000 dollars at a cost of less than $20,000. Bill was elected and served for 23 years in the state senate. He became an important conservative leader, not only in California but nationally.

In the mid-1970s, Richardson visited me in my Tysons Corner, Virginia, office. He wanted me to help him promote a book he had recently written, *What Makes You Think We Read the Bills?* I told him that spending any significant amount of time promoting the book was not a good use of his or my time. I suggested he use direct mail to start and lead a national conservative organization. Thus, Gun Owners of America and Gun Owners of California were born that morning in my office, and within a few years the two organizations had over 350,000 donors/supporters. Almost 50 years later, they are still going strong under the leadership of Tim Macy.

3. How Direct Mail Helped G. Gordon Liddy Run for Congress and Change American and World History

In 1967, I started raising money for an unknown assistant district attorney in Dutchess County, New York—G. Gordon Liddy. He had received a fair amount of local fame by fighting illegal drugs and Timothy Leary, a proponent of them.

I wrote a letter that mailed nationally to hundreds of thousands of conservatives based on fighting crime and illegal drugs. Our mailing included a window decal in the shape of a STOP sign with copy that said, "STOP CRIME, VOTE G.

GORDON LIDDY." We raised hundreds of thousands of dollars nationally and used the money to blanket the congressional district with voter mailings.

Liddy lost a close primary contest to Hamilton Fish IV. The Fish family had represented the congressional district in Congress for almost 100 years.

While Liddy lost the Republican nomination, he won the right to appear on the November ballot as the candidate of the new New York Conservative Party. The New York Republican political leaders were so concerned that Liddy would get enough votes running on the Conservative Party voting line to defeat their candidate, they offered him a position in Washington, D.C., working in the Treasury Department.

He withdrew from the race, came to Washington, D.C.— and the rest is well-recorded in the history books.

The unreported part is that without a big direct mail campaign, Gordon would not have been a serious candidate and almost certainly Republican leaders would not have paid much attention to G. Gordon Liddy—"Now you know the rest of the story" (with thanks to Paul Harvey).

4. Launching the Right to Work Legal Defense Foundation

In 1968, Reed Larson founded the National Right to Work Legal Defense Foundation—a 501(c)(3). In late 1969, George McDonald, a friend and a co-founder of Young Americans for Freedom asked me if I wanted to share the risk on a mailing for the National Right to Work Legal Defense Committee.

I agreed, and we mailed 500,000 letters signed by Arizona Congressman Sam Steiger in early December 1969. Around December 18, a few return envelopes arrived and each day a few more, so that by Christmas Eve we had only around 20 return envelopes with checks. Needless to say, I didn't have a relaxed, carefree Christmas.

December 26 was a Friday. The postman showed up with a big mailbag with return envelopes and each mail day for a month thereafter he was loaded down with bags of mail for the foundation.

When all of the returns were in, the mailing brought in about 300% more than its cost and the Foundation had about 40,000 new donors. They are still going strong over 50 years later under the leadership of Mark Mix.

5. Direct Mail Launched a Future Conservative Star: Phil Crane

When Richard Nixon became president in 1969, he selected 37-year-old Congressman Donald Rumsfeld of Illinois to be his director of the Office of Economic Opportunity.

About eight or nine Republicans filed to run in the primary to be the Republican candidate in the special election to fill Rumsfeld's vacant House seat. A little-known conservative college professor, Phil Crane (Hillsdale graduate), filed as a candidate and asked me to raise money nationally for him.

I said I would, under one condition. All the money we raised had to be spent on voter mailings we would write. This was because only 10–15% of a TV or radio ad would be seen by someone in Phil's congressional district, since there were about eight congressional districts in the Chicago TV and radio market, and we only wanted to talk to registered Republican voters in the district, which would be about 3–4% of the TV and radio audience.

We raised enough money nationally to mail four mailings to every registered Republican voter in the thirteenth congressional district. On Election Day, Phil came in first in the primary, was elected in the general election in 1969, and served 36 years in the House of Representatives.

I especially remember one voter mailing was what I call a "wife letter." It was a three- or four-page handwritten letter on feminine-looking, colored stationary from Phil's wife, Arlene. I enclosed a family photo. Arlene told me that years later people would still come up to her and mention the letter.

6. Senator Jesse Helms Uses Direct Mail to Help Lead the New Right

Jesse Helms was elected to the U.S. Senate in November 1972. In March 1973, his friend, principled political advisor and campaign manager Tom Ellis, called me and said that Helms had a $90,000 campaign debt and did I think I could raise some money to help pay off the debt?

I told Tom that I could mail two letters to a list of about 35,000 high-dollar conservative donors, and after the results of both mailings were received, the debt would be paid, and there would be about $30,000 left over. He told me to go to the Senate and tell that to Helms. I did, and months later, when all the money was received, the debt was paid and about $30,000 was left in the bank.

That opened wide Tom's eyes to what direct mail could do. I soon signed a contract with Helms's political action committee, The Congressional Club. Shortly thereafter the name was changed to the National Congressional Club and quickly became a major player in the conservative movement, congressional battles, and political races through the 1990s.

The club freed Helms of needing the support of Big Government Republicans, as grassroots conservatives financed his campaigns, and he was able to bypass the national Republican Party and Big Media. A key factor in the National Congressional Club's success was their executive director, Carter Wren, who remains active in North Carolina politics today.

In the second half of the 1970s, Senator Helms was the most visible and important elected conservative, and if the Democrats had been able to defeat Helms for re-election in

1978, it would have put a serious damper on Ronald Reagan's 1980 presidential campaign.

The political world, including the liberal media, was watching to see if the New Right had any political strength or if we were a paper tiger. The answer came loud and clear on Election Night November 7, 1978, when Helms was re-elected and three New Right Senate candidates each defeated a Democrat incumbent—Gordon Humphrey beat Tom McIntyre in New Hampshire, Roger Jepsen beat Dick Clark in Iowa, and Bill Armstrong beat Floyd Haskell in Colorado.

The New Right had arrived, and we planted our flag in the middle of the political wars.

By the way, any list of unsung conservative heroes must include Tom Ellis. Most grassroots conservatives have never heard of Tom, but we all stand on his shoulders for many reasons, including he was the brains and drive behind the election of three of the best U.S. Senators in the twentieth century—Jesse Helms, John East, and "Lauch" Faircloth.

Ronald Reagan may have never been nominated for president in 1980 if not for the work of Tom Ellis and Jesse Helms in 1976. Reagan had lost the first six primaries/caucus in 1976 (Iowa, New Hampshire, Massachusetts, Vermont, Florida, and Illinois).

The next primary was North Carolina on March 24, to be followed by Texas five weeks later. Tom told the Reagan Campaign team, don't come into North Carolina to campaign; we will handle everything. However, if you insist on campaigning in North Carolina, you must agree to four things: you must attack the giveaway of the Panama Canal, Henry Kissinger, *Détente*, and President Ford. Reagan and his team agreed and, in an upset, won the primary 52%–48%.

My friend Jeff Bell told me that he was on the Reagan plane after they had finished campaigning in North Carolina on their way to Wisconsin and some had drafted a withdrawal speech for Reagan to give when they arrived in Wisconsin. However, when they landed and learned they had won North Carolina, of course the speech was never given.

If Reagan had lost North Carolina, it's doubtful that he could have kept his campaign going until May 1 (five weeks later) when Texas held its primary and he carried every Texas county.

Once again, Jesse Helms's Congressional Club's use of direct mail advanced the conservative cause and impacted American history.

7. Defeating Common Situs Picketing Legislation

In 1975, Reed Larson of the National Right to Work Committee called and asked me to meet with him to design a campaign to defeat legislation that the Democrats were proposing called Common Situs.

Common Situs was legislation that was of great importance to union bosses. It would allow all the unions involved in a project to go on strike if one union went on strike. In a building project, if one union goes on strike, such as the pipe fitters, all of the other unions on the project are required to keep working.

Union bosses knew their power would be greatly increased if the entire building project could be shut down.

President Gerald Ford promised his secretary of Labor and the union bosses, including George Meany, president of the AFL-CIO, that if the Democrats controlling Congress passed the legislation, he would sign it.

Around September 1975, when I met with Reed in his office on K Street, Washington, D.C., he asked me to put together four million right-of-center names and addresses and write and mail them a letter with postcards for the recipient to mail to President Ford, as well as extra postcards for family and friends. The letter also urged phone calls to President Ford.

A friend, John Carlson, who was a press aide to President Ford told me that the White House received 720,000 post-cards, letters, and phone calls demanding that Ford veto the legislation.

Ford was about to face Ronald Reagan in a battle for the Republican nomination for president. In January 1976, Ford broke his word to the unions and his Secretary of Labor John Dunlop and vetoed the Common Situs legislation. The Republican members of Congress upheld his veto.

The 4 million letters cost about $1 million and about $700,000 came back from the mailing from about 90,000 donors.

Reed went to his grave in 2016, and I will go to mine, not knowing how much these 90,000 new donors gave to the National Right to Work Committee and the Foundation over the next 40 years, but it was probably north of $30 million.

The purpose of the mailing wasn't to make money to run ads in the *Washington Post* or the *New York Times*. It was to pressure Ford to veto the legislation—mission accomplished.

8. Ronald Reagan and the Giveaway of the Panama Canal

In the second half of the 1970s, the giveaway of the Panama Canal was a huge issue. In fact, it was one of the three or four issues that built the modern conservative movement. It played a major role in Ronald Reagan's campaign for president in 1976 and 1980. Twenty-one U.S. Senators (Republican and Democrat) that voted to give away the canal were defeated in the 1978 and 1980 elections.

In the summer of 1977, Senator Paul Laxalt and Ronald Reagan met with the chairman of the Republican National Committee, former Tennessee U.S. Senator Bill Brock, who was raising millions of dollars from conservatives to oppose the giveaway of the Panama Canal. Laxalt and Reagan wanted to spend some of the money on opposing the giveaway. Brock refused and someone who was in the meeting said, "Reagan used words he didn't think Reagan knew the meaning of."

Shortly after that, I was asked by Laxalt to raise some money so that he and Reagan could travel around the country campaigning against the giveaway. I quickly raised about $90,000 net from direct mail on a pro-bono basis.

9. Direct Mail Helped Launch Congressman Ron Paul's Political Career

In 1976, Dr. Ron Paul was a baby doctor (Ob-Gyn) practicing in Lake Jackson, Texas (about 50 miles from Houston). Because of a resignation, there was a vacancy in a House of Representatives seat and the election was held in April 1976.

My company did mailings nationally to raise money to pay for voter mailings to registered Republicans in that congressional district. Once again, it made no sense to buy TV or radio time in Houston or in a few mid-city towns. We only wanted to communicate with registered Republican voters. In those days, most Texas voters still registered as Democrats. Once again, one of our most effective mailings we did for Dr. Paul was our "trademark wife letter." They are powerfully effective.

I've always struggled with remembering people's names. One of the tricks the experts tell you is to associate a person's name with something that will trigger a remembrance. When I first heard Dr. Paul's wife's name, I associated it with a former girlfriend. In a mailing of about 100,000 national fundraising letters, I mentioned Ron was married to Susan—wrong girlfriend. Congressman Ron Paul and his wife, Carol, have been married for 65 years. Mrs. Carol Paul was not pleased, but Ron ignored the mistake.

Dr. Ron Paul won the special election in April 1976 but lost in the general election later in November of that year. However, he came back to win the seat in November 1978.

10. Jimmy Carter Attempts to Change Election Laws to Elect Democrats

(Taken from *The New Right: We're Ready to Lead*, pages 61 and 62)

In March of 1977, Jimmy Carter proposed four changes in our election laws.

They would: (1) have the taxpayers finance all congressional elections; (2) allow any voter to vote on election day if they showed up with most any kind of identification; (3) change the Hatch Act to allow federal employees to actively participate in politics; (4) change the U.S. Constitution to allow for the direct election of the president and do away with the Electoral College.

A few weeks later at about 10:15 one night, my phone rang. It was Paul Weyrich.

He said he had just attended a meeting of conservative Republican senators. He said they had come to the conclusion that even though these election law changes would hurt the Republican Party, there was nothing they could do to stop it—most felt that they were ideas whose time had come.

I told Paul that I felt the New Right leaders could develop the strategy to stop Carter's plan.

I also reminded Paul that it was late, that he had awakened me, and that I would call him in the morning.

I called him the next morning, and we decided to have a meeting once a week in my conference room with about 15 key New Right leaders.

We quickly developed our strategy. Then week after week (sometimes we met more than once a week) we developed and implemented our tactics.

[I had recently hired Bill Rhatican as vice president of Public Affairs at the Viguerie Company. Bill had been press aide to several Republican cabinet officers, as well as worked in the press office of President Ford's White House.]

We made mailings to large Republican contributors, asking them to call wavering senators. We arranged for Op-Ed pieces in major newspapers. We held briefings with the press to explain our position. We mailed millions of letters, asking that phone calls, cards, and letters be sent to Congress.

We also used smart public relations wherever we could. For example, Congressmen Steve Symms and Robert Dornan got national coverage in July 1977 with dummy ID cards (the brainstorm of Dick Dingman at a meeting in my conference room) to demonstrate the possibilities for fraud in Carter's instant voter registration plan.

The ID cards each had the photos of either Symms or Dornan but the names of liberal Democrats on the House Administration Committee who supported Carter's plan. The reporters and the photographers loved it, particularly when liberal Committee Chairman Frank Thompson blew his top in public over the IDs.

The *Washington Star* published an enormous five-column photo on page one of the phony IDs, which had been blown up to poster size for a news conference.

On that day, Carter's plan to let anyone vote who turned up at the polls with just about any kind of paper showing he lived in that voting district died.

The liberal National Committee For An Effective Congress was opposed to one portion of the campaign finance bill, and Common Cause opposed Carter's proposed changes in the Hatch Act. So, we worked with both of these liberal organizations in the areas that concerned them.

Senator Paul Laxalt worked with many businessmen to urge them to pressure Congress.

Laxalt agreed to coordinate the effort inside the Senate. He organized and led a successful filibuster that for weeks defeated the best efforts of President Carter, Senate Majority Leader Bobby Byrd, Teddy Kennedy, and other liberals to pass taxpayer financing of the Congressional elections. And on August 2, 1977, the liberals threw in the towel.

This was the New Right at its best.

About 50 of us got together in September 1977 at a dinner at a Capitol Hill Washington, D.C., restaurant to celebrate David's victory over Goliath. Senator Laxalt received an award from us for leading the "inside" effort, and I received a reward for leading the "outside" effort.

Despite four years of Carter's efforts to change the election laws to put the conservatives out of business, not one of his changes ever became law.

This was probably the first major victory of the New Right. A rag-tag group of New Right conservatives had done what Republican senators said could not be done.

We had our first taste of victory. And there was no stopping us now.

U.S. News and World Report said about us in July 1977: "A third force is quietly building a political apparatus that pointedly disregards party labels."

The *New York Times* said in December 1977: "The New Right . . . is more tightly organized, better financed, more sophisticated and more pragmatic than their predecessors."

11. Repeal of the Catastrophic Health Act
In 1988, the Catastrophic Health Act was passed into law with the support of President Reagan and all Republican and Democrat House and Senate leaders. However, less than a year later, the law was repealed. What happened?

To the best of my knowledge, the only Great Society piece of legislation ever repealed was the Catastrophic Health Act. The public rose up and demanded that it be repealed, largely due to a massive direct mail campaign.

Many conservative organizations conducted large mailing campaigns demanding that the legislation be repealed. ATA's clients mailed in excess of 25 million letters demanding it be repealed. Even the liberal National Committee to Preserve and Protect Medicare mailed and joined in with millions of letters.

12. The Defeat of HillaryCare

In 1993, President Bill Clinton appointed his wife, Hillary, to be in charge of passing a massive healthcare program.

Most Republican leaders were opposed to it, but they quickly made their peace with it, feeling it was an idea whose time had come. However, a number of conservative leaders began to plan strategy to defeat the proposed legislation. The number one person leading the effort was Bill Kristol who, two or three (or more) times each week, sent faxes to thousands of conservative journalists, activists, and leaders outlining problems with the legislation and recommendations of action to take.

I remember being in a room of 300–400 mostly liberals (including Hillary Clinton) in December of 1993. There was a panel of 11 people, 10 of them from the Clinton administration and another from the insurance industry. Of course, all of the Clinton appointees were supportive of the legislation, and the insurance representative was about 60% in support.

The attitude in the room was, "This is a done deed— the legislation will be passed and signed into law shortly." I thought to myself, *These people have no idea what the conservative movement has planned.*

Again, my company mailed over 20 million letters in opposition to the proposed legislation. We mailed for our client, The American Conservative Union, 13 million letters signed by Senator Bob Dole in 100 days. Each letter urged people to contact their U.S. Congressman and two Senators.

In an October 3, 1994, *New York Times* article by Adam Clymer, Mrs. Clinton said, "This battle was lost on paid media and paid direct mail." The legislation was so unpopular at the grassroots that no committee hearing was held in either the U.S. House of Representatives or the U.S. Senate. Mrs. Clinton also said, "If you don't even know about the direct mail campaign, the people who are being influenced by that kind of opposition are going to remain influenced."

One of the major benefits and strengths of direct mail is it flies under the radar of the establishment, including the mainstream media.

13. The Launching of Judicial Watch

In late 1996, Larry Klayman, an attorney, called me and asked to meet. We had breakfast in Washington, D.C., a few days later to discuss raising money for a new organization he had recently founded, Judicial Watch. I had been reading about Judicial Watch in the newspapers and was thinking about calling him.

Judicial Watch had one donor—Klayman—who had lent the organization a substantial sum.

We signed a contract and began writing to conservatives nationally without much success for the first eight to nine months, testing various issues that Judicial Watch was interested or involved in. About the tenth month of mailing, we hit the motherload (with focus on the Clintons, the Whitewater scandal, etc.), and within three years we had developed 330,000 donors for Judicial Watch. Today, under the leadership of Tom Fitton, Judicial Watch is one of the conservative movement's most important organizations and raises close to $200 million a year.

14 Ed Feulner Got to Keep His Job

Around 2011, I was speaking at FreedomFest, a large gathering of libertarians in Las Vegas, Nevada. I was making the point that because of the excesses of the Obama administration and the rise of the Tea Party, it was an excellent time to grow conservative organizations.

In my remarks, I said that if you are leading a conservative organization and you don't double the size of your organization in the next 12–18 months, you should resign.

In the audience was my friend Dr. Ed Feulner, president of Heritage Foundation, and later we chatted about the opportunities to grow conservative organizations.

In December of that year at a Heritage Foundation Christmas Party, Ed came up to me and said that Heritage had grown their number of donors from about 300,000 to 700,000 donors that year, and—based on what I'd said in Las Vegas about doubling the size of his organization—could he keep his job?

15 A Vice President at Our Company Learned Direct Mail and Built a Media Empire

In April of 1962, Tom Phillips, a sophomore at Dartmouth, invited me to bring my new bride to Dartmouth and speak to the young conservatives there. That was the beginning of a lifelong friendship.

Around 1973, Tom was a junior executive at the Leo Burnett Advertising Agency in Chicago and periodically would call to ask if he could come work for me. One day he showed up in my office with his wife of several weeks, and I told him to go down the hall where there was an empty office and I'd catch up with him later. Over the next few years, we launched several newsletters, including the "Pink Sheet on the Left" and the "Retirement Newsletter."

Around 1977, Tom said he wanted to leave the company and start a newsletter business, and he would like to have our two newsletters. I was sorry to see Tom leave but was happy to get rid of the newsletters because that was not part of our core business. In hindsight, I should have said: "Sure,

Tom, you can take the newsletters, I just want 10% of your new company."

Tom pyramided those two newsletters into a large international media company, which employed and then launched direct marketing careers of dozens of young conservatives. Tom sold his company years later for hundreds of millions of dollars.

18

Are You Being a Good Steward of Your Nonprofit's Money?

Do you think the purpose of direct mail is only to raise money?

If so, you are like many (maybe most) conservative leaders.

However, you would not only be wrong, you would be making a huge mistake.

Without the U.S. Post Office, there would be no conservative movement worthy of the name.

In today's "cancel culture" and with Big Media and Big Tech censorship, direct mail plays a significant role in getting news to Americans.

Direct Mail Made the Conservative Movement Possible

In the 1960–70s, hundreds of conservative organizations were launched with direct mail as the primary way they raised their budget, got members and subscribers, sold books and magazines, communicated with their supporters, got publicity, etc. This was necessary before the arrival of the internet, email, Rush, Fox, etc.

What was true in the 1960–70s, is still true today. In fact, the Post Office is more important than ever to conservatives, because our enemies control the high ground of most all major means of communication.

Direct Mail

Yes, direct mail raises money for most all conservative organizations, including finding/identifying people who will become regular donors, monthly donors, major donors, and bequest donors. However, direct mail does many other things that are as important, or more so, than just raising money for conservative causes, organizations, and candidates.

From the 1960s through about 2010, direct mail was the second-largest form of advertising. Today it's the third largest (behind internet and TV). It's important to realize that when you spend money on acquisition/prospect mail to tell people about your organization or the problem your nonprofit was established to solve, it's similar to spending money for advertising on TV, radio, newspapers, magazines, or on a billboard, bumper sticker, etc. Except that the money spent advertising on TV, radio, etc., is almost always gone for good and you don't know who watched your ad and you certainly don't have their name and address to contact them.

However, most of the cost of a postal direct mail is paid for by those who read your letter and liked it so much they sent money and gave you their name and address.

I sometimes hear nonprofit executives question the high costs of direct mail, and whether they are being a good steward of their organization's money when they send acquisition postal advertising letters and receive 60–70% of the cost back from those who receive the ad, as well as their contact information, including sometimes a phone number and email address.

By proper treatment of your new supporters, they will send you more money (often again and again) so that soon the money you invested in the acquisition/prospect direct mail advertising will be totally paid for, which means you conducted a free advertising campaign. You can't do that with TV, radio, billboards, yard signs, bumper stickers, etc.

Many nonprofit executives never question whether they are being good stewards of their organizations' money when they spend money on a TV campaign to promote their cause or a project and receive no money back and no names and addresses of new supporters.

And far too many focus only on high-dollar donors and fail to understand the importance and value of small-dollar donors. One of the reasons the Left is competitive with conservatives on Election Day—even though they are defending failed, terrible policies—is because they understand small-dollar donors are their "army."

Not only do nonprofit executives make these mistakes, but so do members of boards of directors and major donors. Too many are biased against direct mail—they may have fallen for the old saying, "It's junk mail." Junk mail is advertising you're not interested in.

An unsolicited direct mail letter arrives from a candidate for the U.S. Senate that you've never heard of, but you like her position on the issues, she is running a good campaign against a liberal you want defeated, and so you decide to rush a donation via her website. No one in this situation would think of the letter as junk mail.

Most GOP Consultants Misuse Direct Mail

But of all conservative/Republicans who misuse direct mail, none are more guilty than political candidates, their campaign teams, and especially their high-priced campaign consultants.

Political campaign consulting is a big business. Unfortunately, too many campaign consultants are not professional. Most learn by trial and error, by working as a junior aide in a campaign right out of college. Few have spent much time reading and studying about their profession. Most have probably never read a marketing book, which means they have no real understanding of building a BRAND for their candidate.

Also, Republican campaign consultants are well-known as not having strong ideological beliefs. Morton Blackwell says, "Most are content-free"—going with whoever pays them the most. With few exceptions, they resist using principled conservative issues in the campaign. Campaigning as a full out-and-out conservative makes most Republican consultants nervous.

The national Republican committees, including the Republican National Committee, the Senatorial and House of Representative Committees, the Republican Governors Association, etc., are all well-known to be under the control of Big Government, establishment Republicans—many are anti-conservative.

The more paid advertising the campaign does, the more money the consultants make, even if that's not the best use of the campaign's donations.

Most Republican political consultants (I assume the same is true for Democrats) are like a groundhog—they know one thing. And that one thing is a campaign needs lots of money to run lots of ads, for which they are compensated by receiving about 15% of the cost of the ad.

Democrat campaigns generally have strong ground games—thanks to unions and leftwing activists. Few Republican campaigns know what constitutes a ground game, and they seldom have a credible, serious one. To consultants, door knocks and robo phone calls is a good ground game. Also, campaign consultants haven't figured out how to send a 15% invoice for a ground game.

Direct Mail Can Help Create Brand Loyalty

And when a political campaign does do direct mail, it's almost always weak and ineffective. Most political direct mail consists of a large broadside mailer, printed front and back on one page of cardstock, with lots of headlines and family pictures. A well-written, four-page letter hand-written from the candidate, the wife/husband or mother, etc., with a 3×5 snapshot, is far more effective than a commercial-looking broadside.

The high-priced consultant tells a young aide the outline of what they want the self-mailer to be. A few days later the trainee comes back with their copy and photos. The consultant makes a few edits, and then it's sent to a printer and an invoice is sent to the candidate for 15% of the cost of the broadside.

And remember, the primary purpose of any conservative nonprofit is not to raise money for salaries, rent, travel, etc. Even though those things are important, it's also important to remember the reason people give donations is to solve the problem that the organization was formed to solve.

I feel strongly you're not only *not* being a good steward of your nonprofit's money, but you are failing your organization, your donors, supporters, and the cause of liberty, if you fail to fully utilize the power of postal direct mail/direct marketing in the Spiritual Civil War the progressives/socialists/Marxists have declared on the cause of liberty/freedom/America.

To be a good steward of a conservative nonprofit, it's vitally important to understand the many purposes and benefits of postal advertising mail, so I will go over them in detail in the next chapter.

There are valuable ways that direct mail will educate, energize, and activate conservatives, so that we will win more elections and govern America.

19

11 Big Mistakes Conservative Leaders Make

I've identified *11 big mistakes* that conservative nonprofit leaders make that significantly contribute to conservatives having small organizations and weak fundraising compared to Democrats.

Change, as each of us knows, is hard. It will be difficult for conservative leaders of nonprofits to make the changes I write about in this chapter. For some, it's beyond their capabilities—it just won't happen.

Most people walk into the future backwards facing the past. The future is scary. Even though the past and the present are filled with problems—often the devil we know is not as scary as the devil we don't know.

I've said for many years, conservatives are like the biblical Jews who had to wander through the desert for 40 years until that generation of failed/flawed leaders had passed from the scene. And our failed/flawed leaders include not only Republican politicians but many who lead conservative organizations.

Conservatives are not going to get to the political promised land until they get lots of new organizations led by young leaders.

This means if we are to be competitive with the Left and save America and Western Civilization, we need to not only replace most elected establishment Republican politicians with principled, warrior-type conservatives but also the leaders of many conservative nonprofits need to be replaced if they don't quickly make changes.

Also, members of the boards of directors of conservative nonprofits and major donors need to step up and demand results from many weak and ineffective leaders of those conservative organizations.

Grassroots conservatives in 2022 and 2024 will be replacing ineffective, silent, Republican politicians in the primaries. So, why shouldn't the same standard apply to conservative nonprofit executives?

The days of "see, hear, speak no evil" of conservative leaders should be over. Our liberties hang by a thread, and if leaders are not prepared to be effective, be bold, and take risks, hopefully they'll be retired or moved aside.

Here, in no particular order, are the 11 big mistakes executives of conservative nonprofit organizations make.

1. Lack of a Development Team/Department

Most conservative organizations rely almost entirely on direct marketing fundraising: postal, email, phone, and no personal one-on-one solicitation. I tell our prospective clients that 90–95% of ATA's fundraising value is to identify the names of people who, with proper treatment through a development person/department, will contribute 10, 50, 100, or 1,000 times more than through the mail.

Direct mail has been both a blessing and a curse for conservatives. The blessing is obvious—it allows conservatives to go around the mainstream media and build and fund our nonprofits, get subscriptions to our publications, sell books, educate, pass/defeat legislation, identify activists, get votes, etc. The curse is it has caused too many leaders of nonprofits to become armchair generals. Instead of building a vibrant, active grassroots organization, they stay in their comfortable offices and rely on postal mail, email, and phones to supply the money to run the organization.

Over the years, I've had far too many clients take this type of approach: "Hey, Richard. It's Friday morning and you haven't given me any copy to approve this week." Instead of building and operating a real nonprofit, they run a direct mail operation, achieving about 10% of what the organization should be accomplishing.

2. Failure to Employ Enough People in Your Development Department

Do you have $100 donors who never receive a personal thank you phone call? Who never get a happy birthday card with a handwritten note? Or a Happy New Year/just-thinking-of-you phone call? Then you don't have enough people in your development department.

For every $1 you invest in a development person, you should receive $10–$20+ in the first year or two, and many times more in years to come.

3. Thinking of Direct Mail as Only for Fundraising

Direct mail is the third largest form of advertising (first is digital; second is TV).

In addition to raising net money from your previous donors, direct mail does many important things in the public policy arena. It . . .

- educates the public.
- helps BRAND your organization.
- helps BRAND your opponents.
- helps pass legislation.
- helps defeat legislation.
- identifies people who will be activists for your cause.

- encourages people to vote for good conservative candidates
- encourages people to oppose liberal candidates.
- identifies people who are not registered to vote and encourages them to register.
- encourages registered voters to vote.
- helps bond donors to the organization and its mission.
- identifies those who will make automatic monthly gifts.
- identifies those who will make regular gifts when solicited via postal, email, phone.
- identifies people who make major gifts.
- identifies those who can and will leave your organization money in their wills/bequests.
- oh, and did I say? . . . it raises lots of money.

4. Not Knowing Your Donors' LTV

If you don't know the Lifetime Value (LTV) of your donors, you have no idea how much money you should invest to acquire a new donor.

Yes, I know it's difficult to determine the LTV—there are so many variables, including you're a new organization and you have no experience with receiving wills and bequests; you don't know how long the average donor will contribute; you don't know how effective your development team will be, etc. But you must make an effort to come away with an average/range, e.g., "somewhere between $100 and $200," or "at least $1,000," and "probably not more than $2,000," etc.

What should you include in your LTV? The answer is—everything.

- Net from regular (usually monthly) postal mailings to your donors

- Net from emails to your donors
- Any net from newsletters
- Monthly giving programs
- Major gifts
- Wills/bequests
- Income from rental or exchange of your donor file
- Income from fundraising dinners, receptions, etc.
- Etc., etc.

Of course, only part of the LTV of your donors/supporters consists of the donations they give you.

When considering your LTV, keep in mind the purpose of your organization and the value of all the benefits from your mailings that I listed in number three in this chapter, including education, building your BRAND, BRANDING your opponents, passing or defeating legislation, etc.

5. Lack of Significant Investment in Acquiring New Donors

I think we can all agree that few conservative organizations are spending enough money on acquisition when the Left has 700% more donors than conservatives. And why is this? Well, there are a number of reasons.

Lack of professionalism by conservative fundraisers. Most people fundraising for conservative organizations and candidates may have read one or two marketing books, may have attended a few lectures on fundraising, and with good reason they lack confidence in their ability to market aggressively.

Most conservative fundraisers, when I ask how they learned to do their job, reply something along this line, "I watched and studied my boss," "My gut tells me what to do," "I learned by trial and error." My reply to that is, would you go to a doctor or lawyer who learned by trial and error or by the seat of their pants?

Failure to accept a short-run loss in order to have a long-term gain. Farmers know that you plant good seed in one season and harvest lots more seed in another.

Not being willing to take money out of the budget this year and have it returned in the future. If you have a professional in charge of your marketing, all of your acquisition investment will be returned within six to 20 months just from postal mailings to the new donors. So, in a short period of time the cost to acquire a new donor will be zero.

Again, think about a farmer who puts one kernel of corn in the ground, and from that one kernel a corn stalk grows and produces thousands more kernels of corn from that one seed.

Organization leadership that doesn't like direct mail/direct marketing. In this case, I would urge them to read and study the ideas in this book. There's not much else you can do. Life is too short to spend any significant amount of time trying to get them to change their mind. If you find yourself with this situation, decide to spend your time and money with people who want to win and are smart. Remember the saying, "You can't fix stupid." And I don't really mean they're stupid or dumb, but perhaps they are in the category that Rush Limbaugh called "low-information people."

6. Overemphasis on High-Dollar Fundraising

Overemphasis on high-dollar fundraising is killing the conservative movement. Most conservative organizations only want $100+ donors and actually their main emphasis is on $1,000+ donors.

BIG MISTAKE.

Dr. Ed Feulner, former president of the Heritage Foundation, has been a friend since the mid-1970s, and he agrees he had an indispensable partner in building Heritage and that was John

Von Kannon, affectionally known as the Baron because of his last name Von Kannon.

Cancer took John from us in 2016, far too young at age 66. In the early years of the Obama presidency, Ed and John built Heritage donors up to 700,000 last 12-month donors.

Here's a few things Baron and Heritage shared that speak to the importance of acquiring "small-dollar" direct mail donors.

A. "Almost half of Heritage's six-figure-plus donors began their relationship with Heritage with a check of $100 or less in response to a low-dollar direct mail appeal."
B. Some 67% of Heritage major gift donors started in a direct mail program.
C. Two-thirds of their major donors started with a low dollar gift.
D. "Of the nearly $2 billion that Heritage has raised since its founding, 18% of that has come from 50 donors whose initial total combined giving was *less than $2,000*."
E. Heritage's lifetime value of a $20–$30 donor is $400+. About half of a donor's value comes in the first four to five years. The other half comes at the end with major gifts/bequests.
F. Heritage's fundraising is built on a three-legged stool.
   a. Direct Mail
   b. Major Gifts ($10,000+)
   c. Planned Giving

In the last 10 years, Heritage has received donations from over one million individuals. In other words, the more postal donors an organization has, the more major donors they are likely to have.

7. Lack of a Serious Written Plan

As I said before, my heritage is Cajun. Ask a Cajun chef how to prepare any Cajun dish, and he or she will start with the same sentence, "Well, first you make a roux (a sauce)." My advice before starting any important project is, "Well, first you start with what I call Newt's Four-Part Plan" (see Chapter 6).

Before starting any important project, you need to clearly understand where you want to go—where do you want to be in one, five, ten, and twenty+ years? The number one benefit of writing the plan is not working the plan. That's important, but it is secondary. The number one benefit is *writing the plan,* because as you write the plan it helps to clarify your thinking. I do this exercise once or twice a week—before an important meeting, trip, phone call, etc.

I've worked with very few people who understand how to write a plan. For most people a plan is a list of their goals, dreams, wishes, and aspirations. That's not a plan. A plan has concrete measurable actions you're going to undertake to achieve goals, plus when and how.

8. Lack of Professionalism among Those Doing Direct Mail/Marketing

I have said many times, I wouldn't dream of flying in an airplane with a pilot who had the pilot skills of the average nonprofit marketer.

The lack of professionalism among conservative marketers is shocking. The Left has far more top-level, professional marketers than the Right.

9. Lack of a Specific Need/Project for a Donation

The vast majority of fundraising appeals for conservatives, liberals, Republicans, Democrats, charities, health and welfare, etc., are what I call "cuss" letters. Instead of carefully explaining the problem and identifying your solution to the problem, most nonprofits tell us about the problem and then say, ergo send me money. For example . . .

- Democrats are doing bad things, send us money.
- Cancer is a terrible disease, send us money.
- Heart disease is the number one killer of Americans, send us money.
- There's great poverty in X place, send us money.
- Young people are losing their faith in God, send us money.

Your goals, dreams, hopes, wishes, aspirations are not projects.

Yes, donors know there are problems, and they are anxious to help solve the problems, but why should they send *your* organization a donation rather than another organization that offers an exciting specific solution to the same problem?

10. Lack of a Strong Brand
See Chapters 2, 3, and 4.

11. Ineffective/Weak Board of Directors
Most conservative organizations do not have a serious board of directors. Too many conservative leaders lack the confidence needed to run a large organization. Because they lack the proper skills, they have a board of directors composed of a few family members or friends who will not seriously challenge their lack of effective leadership.

If the organization doesn't have a strong board, the leadership will lack serious accountability.

If you're on the board of directors of one or more conservative organizations, do you have the right person leading the organization? And for most conservative organizations the answer is clearly, no.

If you think you have strong leadership, why does your organization only have 5,000, 10,000, or 20,000 last 12-month donors, members, subscribers, while your liberal counterparts have 50,000, 100,000, 300,000+ and budgets that are 500–1,000% + larger than yours?

If you are a major donor and/or on the board of directors of a conservative nonprofit with cautious, timid, low-energy leadership, push them to quickly change or they should be fired, retired, and replaced with mostly younger, bold, energetic conservatives (preferably under the age of 40).

Usually, the real answer as to why conservatives don't invest more in acquisition is some combination of the above.

20

Going Big Safely within the Law
By Mark Fitzgibbons, Esq.,
President of Corporate Affairs
at American Target Advertising, Inc.

If you wish to (1) run for local office (like the school board or a state legislative office) so you can make a difference, (2) help launch the political career of someone, (3) start an organization to have influence on politics and policy, or (4) raise money for your campaign or these other projects, you need to spend the time to study and know at least the basics of the law that governs campaigns and nonprofit advocacy—including getting familiar with some of the lingo. The laws in these areas are overly (and intentionally) complex.

Before you start, it is wise to have a lawyer assist getting your campaign or organization formed. Getting help from a lawyer may be expensive (and this chapter is not legal advice), but activists can at least use the resources identified in this chapter to get a start in local and state politics and policy activism.

Before Throwing Your Hat in the Ring . . .

Candidates for statewide or local elections are under their own state's campaign regulation system.* Often—but not always—the top election official for statewide elections is the secretary of state. The "Find My State or Local Election Office Website" (www.usa.gov/election-office) lists by state

---

* Candidates for federal office are under the jurisdiction of the Federal Election Commission (FEC).

the officials who oversee things like filing to run for office and reporting your campaign finances.

The best resource for conservatives who wish to learn how to run for a state or local office (and to engage in activism generally) is Leadership Institute Training (https://www.leadership institute.org/training/), which provides both online and live seminars throughout the country such as:

- Candidate and Campaign Workshops
- Campaign Management Workshops
- School Board Municipal Candidate and Campaign Academy
- School Board Training

If you wish to run for a state or local office, before you march in parades and kiss your first baby:

- Give your campaign committee a name (e.g., Mark Fitzgibbons for School Board).
- Obtain a tax ID number from the IRS, which may be obtained online at the IRS Online EIN website (search terms: IRS EIN tax application). Once your committee has a tax ID number, it may open a bank account.
- Officially register your campaign and get on the ballot, which may include a declaration of candidacy filed with the state election office, a petition of registered voters, a statement of organization of your campaign, and more. Check your state's requirement at "Find My State or Local Election Office Website" shown above.
- Recruit a treasurer and settle on an official address for your campaign committee.

The rules for campaign finance reporting are rather detailed and complex, so you should read your state's rules before you start—even if you have a good election lawyer and advisors to brief you about what to do to run for office. For example, Virginia provides online a Summary of Laws and Policies [for] Candidate Campaign Committees at https://www.elections.virginia.gov/media/formswarehouse/campaign-finance/2020/Candidate-Summary-2020-09-29.pdf. It will take you from what you must do to get on a state or local election ballot, to campaign finance reporting, to required disclosures on your campaign materials.

The Virginia Department of Elections, for example, has an entire website with Candidate Information (https://www.elections.virginia.gov/candidatepac-info/) explaining the steps one must take to become a candidate, then report.

Are You the Next "Living Room Kingmaker"?

There are strict rules governing corporations or nonprofit organizations hosting events for candidates. What if, however, you want to use your own living room to help launch the political career of a friend, associate, or someone from your church? Everyone surely has heard the story of how Barack Obama got his start in Illinois state politics at a gathering in the home of '60s radicals Bill Ayers and his wife, Bernardine Dohrn.

By way of example, for federal candidates the Federal Election Commission (FEC) excludes "up to $1,000 per candidate, per election for food, beverages, and invitations to host a campaign event that is held in the individual's home, church, or community room." But state laws do not follow the FEC. Clearly if an event were more elaborate than a small gathering, and was advertised as a fundraiser—for example, a plated dinner or reception with a bar and wait staff—the campaign would report that as an in-kind contribution or pay costs incurred. A candidate for state or local office may wish to play it safe, and report the costs of any event, no matter how small, when the rule is not apparent.

Affecting Politics and Policy by Starting an Organization
The three types of private citizen-formed entities that are used most to engage in advocacy are 501(c)(3)s, 501(c)(4)s, and political action committees (PACs). One might even make Referendum/Ballot Initiative Committees a top fourth. This chapter will focus on just C3s and C4s.

If you don't yet have the funds to hire a lawyer to start your organization, there are multiple online resources to help you get started, including LegalZoom (https://www.legalzoom.com/business/business-formation/nonprofit-overview.html) (which is limited to forming C3s), RocketLawyer.com, and even the Left's Alliance for Justice page (https://nlihc.org/sites/default/files/2014-conf-6c.pdf) "Starting a 501(c)(4) Organization." No matter the type of tax-exempt entity you choose, the basics of forming an entity include:

- Creating a nonstock corporation, which requires having Articles of Incorporation and filing the appropriate forms in your state.
- Obtaining a tax ID number from the IRS.

Because the Left relies so much on nonprofit organizations, some of the better-written materials about the rules come from them. Bolder Advocacy, a program of the Alliance for Justice, has an online Resource Library (https://bolderadvocacy.org/resource-library/) with over 400 explanations of rules for both federal and state nonprofit activity.

Example of the Different Purposes of C3s versus C4s
A group of concerned conservatives wish to raise money to create a website providing training materials for other

parents around the state to fight Critical Race Theory in schools. They might create a 501(c)(3) organization, and call it the "Parents Against CRT Education Fund." Or, they may want to create an organization to use grassroots lobbying for or against legislation in the state legislature. They may wish to create a 501(c)(4) organization called "Parents Against CRT Action."

Note: 501(c)(3) and 501(c)(4) organizations obtain their federal tax-exempt status from the IRS, but PACs do not. The IRS has issued several guides such as IRS Publication 557 (https://www.irs.gov/pub/irs-pdf/p557.pdf) with great detail helpful to start nonprofit organizations and comply with the law. The IRS even has online courses called "Starting Out" (https://www.stayexempt.irs.gov/home/starting-out/starting-out) explaining how to apply for C3 and C4 status.

C3s and C4s also file annual tax information returns called Form 990, and by law those returns are available to the general public.

C3s may not engage in partisan politics, but that does not mean they must refrain from discussing issues in the political arena. For example, C3s may be used for voter registration, get out the vote (GOTV), and even hosting candidate debates, but such activities may not be used to favor one candidate or group of candidates. In other words, the "political" activities may not be partisan.

C4s are what are called "social welfare" organizations, and unlike C3s are not completely barred from partisan political activities. C4s must comply with the "primary purpose" test, however, meaning that less than a majority of an organization's activities may be partisan political.

C4s may engage in unlimited lobbying, including asking people to petition legislatures, which is known as grassroots lobbying. Therefore, C4 fundraising materials may include grassroots petitions to legislatures on specific legislation.

C3s and C4s must report annually to the IRS to maintain their tax-exempt status. The annual information return that C3s and C4s file with the IRS is called Form 990. The amount of the annual gross receipts and assets dictates which version of the Form 990 the organization must file.

Attention Start-Ups: When annual gross receipts are $50,000 or less, your organization is eligible to file electronically Form 990-N, called the "e-Postcard," to satisfy its annual reporting requirement. The IRS Form 990-N Electronic Filing System (e-Postcard) User Guide (https://www.irs.gov/pub/irs-pdf/p5248.pdf) explains the steps to register and become eligible for this less burdensome reporting process.

Soliciting donations may require you to register with states. Nearly 40 states (and some local jurisdictions) have what are called charitable solicitation laws that require nonprofits to register annually before they may solicit donations from the public (which includes previous donors). Because too many state charity regulators operate in outdated ways even when they have digitized the annual registration and renewal process, compliance is surprisingly expensive and cumbersome for organizations that solicit donations. If your organization is soliciting donations only within one state, you can easily find the requirements using search terms as "charitable solicitation registration" and your state's name. If you plan to solicit nationally, there are law firms and other professional services available to assist you in registering in multiple states.

The National Association of State Charities Officials (NASCO) has a chart (https://www.nasconet.org/wp-content/uploads/2020/05/NASCO-State-Charities-Registration-Survey-5.15.20-.pdf) showing which states require registration, links to the homepage of the registration office, and the address of the state official with whom registration is made.

A Special Word for Religious Leaders

I strongly recommend that you read the "Politics and the Pulpit Election Articles Series" by one of my heroes, Fr. Frank Pavone of Priests for Life, found at this link: https://www.politicalresponsibility.com/elecarticles.htm. In "Part Two: The IRS is Not the Law," https://www.priestsforlife.org/columns/4896-politics-and-the-pulpit-part-two-the-irs-is-not-the-law, Pavone writes, "So many pastors and their congregations are under the impression that they are going to 'violate the law' if they distribute a voter guide or preach about the urgent importance of voting pro-life. Nonsense, and it's time we start saying so. This series of columns will tell you why."

While it is extremely important to follow the law, we should keep in mind that misinterpretations of the civil laws that govern our speech, religious, and other constitutional rights may harm our liberties and our callings to do what's right under God's law. Government officials are periodically (if not often) wrong or even lawless in their interpretations of their power, and should be questioned and challenged.

21

How to Grow 10×=1,000%
By Kathleen Patten,
President and CEO of
American Target Advertising, Inc.

Would you believe that it's easier to grow your organization or your business or you personally by 1,000% rather than by 100%?

The world's best and best-known coach for entrepreneurs is Dan Sullivan, founder and president of The Strategic Coach® Program, a Toronto- and Chicago-based coaching organization for entrepreneurs.

When I first heard Dan Sullivan say it would be easier to grow our company 1,000% than 100%, it didn't make any sense. However, Dan reminded me that we had done it several times previously. And he was right.

Richard Viguerie started the company with one employee and within a few years he had 10, which is a 1,000% increase. A few years later he had 100 employees, again a 1,000% increase. Then a few years after that, 250 employees.

Richard joined Dan's Strategic Coach program in 2003, and I have been in Dan's program since 2010.

In different places in *GO BIG* Richard stresses the importance of having mentors. Of his four mentors, three are deceased; however, the fourth, Dan Sullivan, at age 77, is at the top of his game helping thousands of entrepreneurs grow some part of their business, organization, or life 2×, 5×, 10×, and even more.

So how do you do this? Well, the best way is to join The Strategic Coach program, but since only a few will become a part of The Strategic Coach program, buy and study all of Dan's 12 mini-books available online. You don't read Dan's books once. You underline the parts that resonate with you, then return to the book for a review two, three, or maybe even four times a year to the underlined parts.

Growing 10× is not something most people were born knowing how to do. It isn't normal thinking. The idea of growing 10× is scary and intimidating to most people.

You can't grow 10× by doing the same things you always do. Starting your day a little early or working a little later, putting in more weekends at the office, etc., are all things that can bring you incremental growth, 2× or 3× growth, but not exponential growth.

Leading an organization or a project to exponential growth requires a shift in your mindset. "Your mindset is the most essential tool you have," is another quote by Dan Sullivan. A linear mindset goes from 1 to 2 to 3 to 4 to 5. Exponential growth is simply doubling: 1 to 2 to 4 to 8 to 16 to 32.

To grow 10× you have to make major shifts in your thinking. Major shifts in your business. Major shifts in how you use your time and who you spend it with.

Dan Sullivan says, "If you want to be great, make the extraordinary normal."

You don't naturally know how to grow exponentially any more than a cardiac surgeon naturally knows how to perform open heart surgery. Cutting people open is abnormal behavior. The surgeon trains himself or herself to do something abnormal. Through that training, the skills and thinking become normal to them. And he or she can do something extraordinary that most others never will.

So how do you change your mindset?

Seven Things to Have 10× (1,000%) Growth

1. **Courage.** In Strategic Coach®, one of Dan Sullivan's books, *The 4 C's Formula: Commitment, Courage, Capability, and Confidence*, talks about the "building blocks of growth." Notice how courage comes *before* you have developed the capabilities and before you gain the confidence. You need to make the commitment to 10× growth and have the courage to start. Once you do those two things, the capabilities and confidence will follow.

2. **The 80–20 Rule.** The Pareto Principle (https://www. investopedia.com/terms/p/paretoprinciple.asp) outlines how 20% of effort or input equals 80% of results. Identify for yourself and your organization what that 20% is. Cal Newport's excellent book *Deep Work* emphasizes the value of intense focus. Identify the 20% that will generate 80% of your growth and then do a deep dive focusing on that subject. For example, if 80% of a nonprofit's income comes from 20% of its donors, how does it exponentially grow the pool of donors? (Read Perry Marshall's book *80/20 Sales and Marketing*).

3. **Find Your Who.** Most people's natural way of thinking is to think tactically. When confronted with problem X, we ask ourselves, *What do I need to do to solve problem X?* Exponential growth only comes when YOU are not solving problem X. You only have so many hours in the day. And you need to focus on what you are uniquely good at. In each situation, look for the "who" that can take the lead on the project, solve the problem for you, write the plan, run the marketing, and so forth. (Read Dan Sullivan's book with Dr. Ben Hardy, *Who Not*

How. The concept is simply life-changing. *See* https://whonothow.com.)

4. **Collaboration**. Collaboration is a true multiplier. Identifying what you are uniquely good at as a company, within terms of people and a business as a whole, is a key focus of Sullivan's coaching program. Once you do that, you have started down a path of success. When two entrepreneurial businesses combine forces on a project, focusing on amplifying their strengths and not focusing on competition, huge things can happen. Together they create opportunities that propel growth and success. Sullivan has a book on collaboration that can be found on Amazon or Strategic Coach's website.

5. **Multipliers**. Peter Diamandis, founder of the X Prize Foundation, said, "The on-ramp for an exponential mindset is asking, *What am I not digitizing that I should be?*" A good example of this is Hillsdale College. Once Hillsdale took their in-person courses (starting with an introduction to the Constitution) online, their reach moved from the 1,500 students on campus each year to hundreds of thousands of Americans across the country each year. Going digital with their online courses and marketing efforts grew their reach much more than 10×. And it keeps growing every year, thanks to the entrepreneurial mindset of Hillsdale College President Dr. Larry Arnn.

6. **Conquering Complexity**. When your growth plateaus, look for what Dan Sullivan calls "ceilings of complexity" in your organization. Where can you simplify things, digitize things, etc.? What are the ceilings of complexity that hold you back from exponential growth?

7. **All of Life**. Look at all aspects of your life, not just your business. Identify what in your life needs to be jettisoned. What will remain? Not just things or activities,

but even people. Surround yourself with people who are entrepreneurs. Most people attracted to right-of-center nonprofits are in it for the project/program. They want to do good. They want to change the world. They usually didn't go to business school and don't know much about building a business. You need to surround yourself with entrepreneurs, risk-takers, people who can guide you and celebrate your successes with you.

Read, read, read. Read everything you can about how to grow your business exponentially. Read all of Dan Sullivan's publications. Again, read Ben Hardy's book with Sullivan, *Who Not How*. Listen to Sullivan's many different podcasts. His company also has a book coming soon titled *10× Is Easier than 2×*. And Ben Hardy's newest book, *Be Your Future Self Now*, is about how to create a bigger future than you can imagine.

By the way, if you're thinking that 10× growth will take even more of your limited time, Sullivan says it's the opposite. A 10× growth plan will allow you to have more free time because of the changes you'll make in your life.

Growing 1,000% doesn't mean you have to grow the number of your employees, your donors, and sales, profits, etc., by 1,000%. You choose what you want to increase 1,000%.

Perhaps it might be increasing your effectiveness 1,000% by January 2024, which is what our company is focusing on. By doubling our employees and focusing on high-level/world-class marketers and adding 20–30 new clients who are led by high-energy entrepreneurs, we will be in a position to increase our impact on American public policy by 1,000%.

Also, by spending 1,000+ hours of Richard's time and 1,000 hours of our team's time in 2022 writing *GO BIG*, it's possible that ATA's impact will be far greater than 1,000% increase.

Think of the impact of thousands of new conservative organizations, each with 5–10 mostly young conservatives learning to be leaders, and each new organization getting thousands or tens of thousands of new donors.

All because of the ideas and encouragement from this new book by Richard Viguerie.

Many of the 5,000 conservative leaders that receive Richard's monthly marketing memos share them with their team members, board members, and donors.

This book will probably be read by tens of thousands of conservatives. Some will use his advice to significantly grow their organization or start a new organization or win an elected office. Also, our 40+ conservative nonprofit clients will send tens of billions of letters, emails, digital ads, radio and TV ads, etc., in the next few years.

So, the impact of American Target Advertising's monthly leadership memos and *GO BIG*—as well as our clients' postal and digital communications, articles, books, etc.—in the next few years means we'll have 1,000%+ more impact than just a few years ago.

And if our ATA team and I can and will do this, you also can have 1× growth soon, followed by 2×, then 4×, and soon you're on your way to 10×=1,000% growth, and probably making a significant contribution to saving America and Western Civilization.

22

American Target Advertising's Past, Present, and Future Role in the Conservative Movement

I'm known by some conservatives as 002, which means I've been active at the national level of the conservative movement longer than every living conservative except for my dear friend Dr. Lee Edwards, a senior fellow at the Heritage Foundation and the lead chronicler of the history of the conservative movement and its leaders through the dozens of books he's written.

I founded the world's first ideological, political, direct mail/marketing agency in January of 1965, with one client (YAF) and 12,500 Barry Goldwater $50+ donors that I got from the clerk of the U.S. House of Representatives.

In the last 57 years, our A team at ATA has mailed over 4.7 billion letters, helped raise almost $8 billion dollars, and acquired 86 million donations for our clients. In 2022, our company is still the world's largest conservative direct marketing agency with 20 clients, over 90 team members mailing over 120 million postal letters yearly, and the names of millions of conservative donors and activists.

In 1965, there were only a few conservative organizations. In those early months, I went to some of them, and they agreed to mail 5,000 test letters. The results were exceptionally good, bringing in 200–300%+ more than the cost of the mailing.

I told the clients that these were great results, and we should quickly mail 50,000 more letters, and if the results come back the same as the test, let's mail 500,000 letters. All said, "No, let's mail another 5,000." My response was usually something like, "Hey, I can see the barbarians. They are just down the street; they will be here soon; we need to quickly build a large conservative movement." But they all said, "No, we'll just mail another 5,000 letters."

By the summer of 1965, I realized that God, in his infinite wisdom, seldom saw fit to put an entrepreneur (i.e., a risk-taker) in a nonprofit body. So, to help build the conservative movement quickly, I began to sign contracts where ATA took on all of the risk. If the money came in, they would pay our bills. If the money did not come in, we took the loss. And based on that model, our company helped conservatives "own" grassroots marketing for the next 20 years.

Today, the ATA team is led by strong and experienced executives, which include our president and CEO, Kathleen Patten; president of Corporate Affairs, Mark Fitzgibbons; president of our List Company (American Mailing List Corporation), Dorothy Miller; vice president of Administration, Vi Shields; myself as chairman; and dozens of others.

Most of our top executives are women. Success in direct mail advertising has nothing to do with your age, gender, race, or ethnicity. The results of the mailings speak for themselves. One of the many things I like about direct mail is you know to the penny the cost of your advertising mail and to the penny how much money was received.

When I started in direct mail in 1961, I selected someone to evaluate my effectiveness, and in the last 60 years, they've never been wrong. Who was this? The postman. If the postman brings a lot of return envelopes, it's a good day. Not many envelopes, not a good day.

In this way, direct mail advertising is very different from general advertising. If Ford Motor Company spends $10 million on a big TV campaign, no one involved will ever know whether they made sales for Ford (and if so, how many) or lost sales.

By the way, I'm referring to direct mail as advertising, because it is the third largest form of advertising in America (first is digital; second is TV). It is advertising just like having an ad on radio or TV, in newspapers, magazines, billboards, bumper stickers, digital ads, etc.

ATA pioneered many ideas commonly used today in political direct mail, including leading with a technique at the beginning of a letter, such as a:

- Survey
- Poll
- Petition
- Coins
- Dollar bill
- Stand-alone photos
- Debt reduction
- Oversized inline self-mailers
- Live check for a small amount of money, e.g., $1 or $2
- Pseudo check for a large amount—check not negotiable

There's a Spiritual Civil War raging in America, and our side is not doing well. The Left is on our 20-yard line, and the only thing standing between the socialists/Marxists and the goal line is conservatives.

Hopefully, national, state, and local conservative leaders will re-think what needs to be done. America is worth taking risks and sacrifices for. At ATA we've decided to move our company to the front lines of the Spiritual Civil War and to help grow the conservative movement.

As part of ATA's plan to help conservatives win this war, we will greatly increase our effectiveness in 2022–2024, including:

ATA's Plan to Have 10× Growth in Effectiveness by 2024

- Double the number of our clients from 20 to 40.
- Grow our team members from 90 to 135.
- Mail 500 million+ postal letters for our clients.
- Acquire 5 million new conservative donors for our clients.
- Raise $1 billion for our clients.
- Continue to conduct free seminars to train future world-class direct marketers.
- Continue to write monthly marketing memos to 10,000 conservative leaders, executives, and major donors.
- Coach our clients and thousands of conservatives on how to have 10× growth, including
    - launching thousands of new nonprofits
    - growing existing nonprofits into giant organizations.
    - significantly growing the number of conservative donors
    - raising billions of dollars
    - winning elections.

This will expand liberty and freedom throughout the world and assign the slavery of liberalism to the ash heap of history.

I'm one of the last people still active at the national level who was there at the beginning of the conservative movement in the early 1960s. I and ATA have helped build the movement once before, and we're going "once more unto the breech, dear friends, once more . . . ." —*Henry V*, Shakespeare.

I know *what* to do and *how* to do it. But since I'm only one person, I'll need to find lots more *whos*. Who will do this, this, and that?

The team members we're mostly in need of (as is the conservative movement) are copywriters, especially prospect copywriters, who can write a direct mail letter that can successfully be mailed to millions of people.

Today there are no more than eight or nine conservatives who fit that description and most work for ATA.

"So, Richard, if there are only eight or nine, and you employee four or five—where will you find more?"

Good question. I'll do what I've done previously—hire very good commercial or charitable copywriters and convert them from selling widgets or raising money for good charities to writing for organizations that will help save Western Civilization.

If you are a retired world-class marketer, sold enough widgets, or raised hundreds of millions of dollars for a good charity, and want to move to the front lines and enlist in the Spiritual Civil War—call my office.

The type of new clients ATA will acquire are ones that are focused on:

- an issue that if not dealt with can put conservatives out of business, e.g., the Democrats' H.R. 1 in 2021–22, on so-called "ballot security," etc.
- issues that can significantly grow the conservative movement by identifying millions of new people who are not currently supporting conservative candidates or causes to become donors. The issues include China, United Nations, border control, term limits, reparations, D.C. and Puerto Rico becoming states, First Amendment (free speech and religious liberty), Second Amendment, law enforcement/defund the police, national security, cancel culture, indoctrination of school children, etc., etc.

Hopefully national, state, and local conservatives will rethink what they should be doing. America is worth taking risks and making sacrifices.

The Republican Party doesn't have the leaders, energy, ideas, or the will to engage the Left in the Spiritual Civil War the Left has launched that will turn America into a one-party, socialist dictatorship. If America and Western Civilization are to be saved, it will be up to us conservatives to provide the leadership.

ATA is rushing to the front lines in this Spiritual Civil War. We look forward to being of help to our fellow conservative warriors in any way we can. If you need us, let us know, but regardless—we'll see you on the battlefield.

"The harvest is plentiful, but the laborers are few"
—Matthew 9:37 (KJV)

23

A Call to Arms

Fellow conservatives, do you realize we are in a Spiritual Civil War?

It's vitally important that you recognize this fact.

Why?

Because it's not possible to win a war you don't know you're in.

Americans with traditional moral values did not realize they were in a cultural war during most of the 1960s–2000, and guess what—we lost it.

When we finally woke up, we found an America that is comfortable with abortion on demand for any reason at any time, same-sex "marriage," biological males in women's bathrooms and sports, couples living together outside of marriage, a hookup society, soft porn in mainstream media, the internet awash in hardcore pornography, schools teaching that America is a racist country, and K–3rd grade children being taught they can change their sex, and they might be a homosexual.

The people who led this cultural revolution are called Democrats, but they are actually elite socialists, and some are Marxists (communists).

Today these same Democrats are close to turning America into a one-party, socialist/Marxist, anti-God, fascist dictatorship.

As I previously observed, these people control every major institution in America (higher education, lower education, Big Media, Big Tech, Big Business, Wall Street, legal community, organized religion, nonprofit community, unions, military, FBI, CIA, IRS, Justice Department, State Department, etc.).

The only thing they don't control is the electors—the voters. About half of the country regularly votes Republican, and in the upcoming November 2022 election, the vote for GOP candidates will probably exceed 55%.

I've given you a lot to digest—some is discouraging, some is positive, even encouraging.

Many people played an important role in the American revolution of 1776 and the war with Great Britain that followed. One was Thomas Paine, whose brilliant writing inspired the American Patriots. In the appendix to his letter, "Common Sense," he wrote:

> We have it in our power
> To begin the world over again.

I paraphrase Paine and say, we conservatives have it in our power to reclaim our great country and re-establish it as "the land of the free and the home of the brave."

You may be thinking there's so much to be done—so little time. Where should I spend my time, talents, energy, money, etc., etc.?

Did you read in school Henry Wadsworth Longfellow's epic poem *Midnight Ride of Paul Revere*?

> Listen, my children, and you shall hear
> Of the midnight ride of Paul Revere
> On the eighteenth of April in '75:
> Hardly a man is now alive
> Who remembers that famous day and year.
> . . .
> And yet, through the gloom and the light,
> The fate of a nation was riding that night;
> And the spark struck out by that steed, in his flight,
> Kindled the land into flame with its heat.

. . .

A cry of defiance and not of fear,
A voice in the darkness, a knock at the door,
And a word that shall echo forevermore!
For, borne on the night-wind of the Past,
Through all our history, to the last,
In the hour of darkness and peril and need,
The people will waken and listen to hear
The hurrying hoof-beats of that steed,
And the midnight message of Paul Revere.

Well, today's America needs millions of Paul Reveres. Because of the bias of most mainstream media and Big Tech (which silences conservatives voice, opinions, values, and information), millions of conservatives are needed to spread the word as Paul Revere and others did to support the revolution.

There are many opportunities to help spread the truth and educate Americans, which will grow the conservative movement, reclaim the culture, win elections that allow conservatives to govern America, and—to paraphrase Ronald Reagan—assign the Left to the ash heap of history.

Where do you see yourself? Some may feel that because they don't run an organization, there's nothing they can do—wrong. However, some will quickly think of something they want to focus on. Others may see two or three or more things they can do. Whether you decide to focus on one thing or many, you can do something.

Remember the great Mississippi River doesn't start with the full force it has when it passes through Minnesota and Iowa, then later Memphis and St. Louis until it empties into the Gulf of Mexico at New Orleans. It starts with millions of drops of water that become thousands of little rivulets of water that fill hundreds of small streams, then larger streams.

Then the streams begin to come together in a small river that grows until it becomes the mighty Mississippi.

The conservative movement began forming in the 1950s, then grew larger in the 1960s, becoming a powerhouse in the 1970s that nominated and elected Ronald Reagan president in 1980. And by the end of that decade America was booming, and the Soviet Union was a shambles.

My back-of-the-envelope list of things conservatives need to reclaim our institutions, our culture, and our country include:

Today Conservatives Need . . .

1. **At least 20,000 new local, state, and national single-issue organizations.** The Left has 20,000, and conservatives have about 1,000–2,000.
2. **New, mostly young (under 40), leaders with entrepreneurial, risk-taking spirits to launch and lead the 20,000 new organizations.** Part of the definition of a leader includes being bold and a risk-taker and getting out of your comfort zone.
3. **A minimum of 100,000 people to help lead the 20,000 new conservative organizations.** Positions include chairman of the board of directors, board members, a president, vice presidents, and secretary/treasurer. Also, people will be needed to handle media, membership recruitment, fundraising, a website, maintaining mailing lists, etc., etc.
4. **A pro-bono attorney for each of the 20,000 organizations.**
5. **Grassroots donors giving $10, $15, $25, $50, $100+.** Don't think your donations won't make a difference. One of the reasons we're losing America is because 20 million liberals are making modest donations that

add up to tens of billions of dollars. Your gift regardless of the amount is important if we are to save America.

6. **Major donors of $1,000+.** By the way, in addition to donating to conservative organizations and candidates, consider contributing money to individuals who need financial help to be a part-time/full-time activist.

7. **Mega donors of $100,000+.** The Left has dozens and dozens of very wealthy people who yearly donate tens or hundreds of millions of dollars to leftwing causes and candidates. Where are the conservatives who give mega donations to support their views and values to grow the conservative movement like these liberals: Mark Zuckerberg, Mike Bloomberg, Jeff Bezos, Mackenzie Bezos, Bill Gates, George Soros, etc.?

8. **Blogs.** Is there a conservative issue you're passionate and knowledgeable about? You can start a blog. You can start small, blogging once a week to your Christmas card list of family and friends. Then if there's a demand, you should increase the frequency and enlarge your audience.

9. **Podcasts.** Some will have an expertise or interest in a public policy area. If so, you should consider sharing with others via a regular podcast.

10. **Emails/texts.** Everyone can regularly forward conservative articles to family, friends, and others. Grandparents should regularly email/forward good conservative material to their grandchildren, nieces, nephews, etc.

11. **Tweets.** Build an e-list of your family, friends, fellow church members, old school friends, etc., and when you read or see in the media that Democrats have done or said something outrageous, tweet and email

to the list and urge them to pass the information on to others. You always, of course, should provide an opportunity for a person to opt-out.

12. **To review FedUpPAC.org and ConservativeHQ.org will daily post articles for you to share.** Also, at the FedUp Website will be videos, e-books, books, sample emails that will help educate non-conservatives.

13. **Social Media.** Post on Facebook, share Instagram stories, send Snapchats, Tweet regularly, post and/or forward YouTube videos to family and friends.

14. **Books.** When you read a good conservative book, don't put it away and forget about it. Give it to someone who will read it and will also pass it on.

15. If it's a particularly good book, **buy more copies and give them away**.

16. **Take action after reading a conservative publication** and don't throw it away. Give it to someone.

17. **Give gift subscriptions to conservative magazines,** such as *Wall Street Journal*, *Washington Times*, *Epoch Times*, Hillsdale's monthly speech digest *Imprimis* (which is free) to your children, grandchildren, nieces, nephews, cousins, etc.

18. **Encourage others to start conservative nonprofit organizations and/or support them.**

19. **Ask all of your family and friends, age 18 and older, if they are registered to vote.** If they haven't voted recently, they may have been removed from the voter rolls. Encourage them to check and confirm that they are registered.

20. **Encourage/push family and friends to vote.**

21. **Sign up to be an election official** so you will be in the room before people start voting, and you'll also be there in the counting of ballots/votes.

22.**Volunteer on Election Day** to turn out the conservative Republican vote.

23.**Put bumper stickers on your car(s).** Get lots of extra bumper stickers and give them away.

Have I left something off my list? If so, let me hear from you. Email me at rav@gobigconservatives.com with your thoughts.

In the coming months I expect to update and reprint *GO BIG*. I welcome your ideas as to how it can be improved.

My list has something for everyone, but nothing happens until *you* take action—put energy into the battle for liberty, freedom, and America.

America needs *you* and *your voice.*

If you found this book helpful, if you think it has value in the Spiritual Civil War raging all around us, order extra copies and give them to family and friends. I've priced it under cost to encourage you to purchase more copies.

I'm sure you've noticed that liberals constantly and loudly speak out, telling one and all their political thoughts and opinions. Not so much with conservatives. We're busy with our families, church, work, community, and volunteering. We generally like to live and let others live their lives also.

Quite frankly, that needs to change if we're to save America.

America needs you to speak out. Share your views, values, opinions with your family, friends, neighbors, co-workers, fellow church members, old school friends, etc., and urge, nudge, encourage, push them to also get involved.

When in the supermarket or some other public or private situation, comment how much more expensive things are now since Biden's been president. Mention to people that gasoline is sky high because Democrats have a war against fossil fuels.

To paraphrase the renowned teacher Charles E. Weller, now is the time for all good men and women to come to the aid of their country and become modern-day Paul Reveres spreading the word that the anti-American elitist social-ists/Marxists are coming.

Why?

Because we are in a Spiritual Civil War.

America is worth an hour a day of your time.

> "When someone has been given much, much will be re-quired in return; and when someone has been entrusted with much, even more will be required"
>
> —Luke 12:48 (NLT).

P.S. Yes, I'm adding a P.S. in a book chapter. In direct mail, you always want to have a P.S., because it's one of the most widely read parts of a letter—and the message in my P.S. is vitally important.

Actually, constitutional, traditional value conservatives are engaged in not one but three wars. However, the purpose of this book is to focus your attention on the most important war—the Spiritual Civil War raging in America. Because if we don't win this Spiritual Civil War, we will certainly lose the other two.

Remember, America fought in two areas in World War II, Europe and Asia. Now once again we have to fight in multiple wars.

The second war is with the one-worlders—the world's elite establishment. Throughout the free world there is an elite (think—United Nations, World Health Organization, European Union, etc.) that wants to set up a new world order with a government they control.

And the third war, of course, is with the totalitarian gov-ernments (Chinese Communists, Russian Communists, Radical Islam) who want to destroy Western Civilization and

Democracy. If that goal is achieved, the dictators will then fight among themselves for "final" control of the world.

Today, our time and talent need to be focused on winning America's Spiritual Civil War. When we win the Spiritual Civil War, we will then have the leaders and resources we need to fight and win the other two world wars.

Acknowledgments

As I say in the Introduction, about every six weeks since December 2017 I write a marketing memo to 10,000 conservative leaders, marketers, activists, and major donors with advice, suggestions, and recommendations as to how to grow conservative organizations, launch new ones, acquire more supporters, raise more money, and BRAND: yourself, your organization, and the Democrats.

I drew heavily on the 33 marketing memos for the contents of *GO BIG*.

Of all of the people I want to acknowledge and thank for helping bring this book into being, the number one is my executive assistant, Meredith Cole. I've been blessed with a number of high-quality executive assistants since I started the company in 1965, including Joan Bennett, Dottie Bradbury, Nancy Bakersmith, Bob Sturm, and now for five years, Meredith Cole.

I never would have thought that I could do my work with an assistant who didn't have an office next to mine, but as the cliché goes—the world is a-changing. Meredith, her husband, and their three young children recently moved to Georgia, and Meredith and I haven't missed a beat.

I edit the average piece of copy I write 10+ times. Meredith is incredibly patient with me. I want to also thank my assistant, Linda Hall, who backed up Meredith when she was consumed with all of my edits.

In addition, I want to thank Kathleen Patten, president and CEO of our company, American Target Advertising, Inc. (ATA); and Mark Fitzgibbons, president of Corporate Affairs of ATA, for keeping the company on its strong growth pattern as I focused on *GO BIG*. Each of them also helped with a chapter, edits, additions, and critiques.

If you find this book readable, it's thanks to Dara Ekanger, who served as my editor, and Charles King, who served as my designer, both highly recommended to me by my longtime friends Jameson Campaigne and Dan Oliver.

Jameson is the conservative movement's premier expert on publishing and marketing books. As he has done previously for some of my books, he took my manuscript and turned it into the book you're now reading or listening to.

A few months ago, I was reviewing some old memos from my friend Kevin Gentry. In one he asked this question, "If we wanted to go big in this area, what would it take?" I immediately said to myself, "That's it—*GO BIG*—that's the name for my book I've been looking for. Thanks, Kevin."

Of course, I couldn't write my monthly marketing memos or this book without the professional people at ATA—thanks, Team, you're the best. Over the last 57 years, you've helped raise almost $8 billion for right-of-center causes and candidates. The survival of Western Civilization and America rests significantly on the work you're doing for our clients, and as President Ronald Reagan said, "You ain't seen nothing yet." We will be on the front lines in the Spiritual Civil War the Left has launched against America, our Constitution, and traditional Judeo-Christian moral values.

Appendix 1

Richard A. Viguerie's
Direct Marketing/Fundraising Suggested Reading List

The Man Nobody Knows by Bruce Barton
Secrets of Successful Direct Mail by Richard V. Benson
Storytelling Can Change the World by Ken Burnett
Influence and Pre-Suasion by Robert B. Cialdini
Purple Cow by Seth Godin
Fund Your Cause with Direct Mail by Benjamin Hart
My Life in Advertising and Scientific Advertising by Claude C.
　　Hopkins
All books by Al Ries and/or Jack Trout
How to Write Successful Fundraising Appeals by Mal Warwick &
　　Eric Overman (plus many other titles by Warwick)
Raising More Money with Newsletters by Tom Ahern
Monthly Giving Made Easy by Erica Waasdorp
America's Right Turn by Richard A. Viguerie and David Franke
　　(Not a marketing book, but it is the only book that chronicles
　　the history of political direct marketing, especially postal mail)

NOTE: Own a copy of each book. Read each at least several
times and highlight the most important parts. Then review
highlighted parts 2–3 times a year.

Highly recommended FREE e-letters/blogs:

- *The Agitator* (www.agitator.thedonorvoice.com/)
- *Kevin Gentry's Weekly Tips*
  (email: kevin.gentry@kochps.com)
- Seth Godin (www.sethgodin.com)
- Brian Kurtz (www.briankurtz.net/blog)

Appendix 2

Conservative Organizations, News, and Learning

Here's a list of high-quality websites, publications, blogs, organizations to help you grow in your political effectiveness, knowledge, speaking, work, and profession:

Conservative Organizations
Where can I go to become more effective?

Advancing American Freedom – Mike Pence's grassroots public policy organization.

Alliance Defending Freedom – The world's largest legal organization committed to protecting religious freedom, free speech, marriage and family, parental rights, and the sanctity of life.

American Conservative Union – The American Conservative Union is a political organization that advocates for conservative policies, ranks politicians based on their level of conservatism, and organizes the Conservative Political Action Conference.

America First Policy Institute – Advances policies that put the American people first. Their guiding principles are liberty, free enterprise, national greatness, American military superiority, foreign-policy engagement in the American interest.

Capital Research Center – Investigative think tank that examines how foundations, charities, and other nonprofit organizations spend money and get involved in advocacy and politics.

CatholicVote – America's largest conservative Catholic advocacy organization whose mission is to inspire every

Catholic in America to live out the truths of their faith in public life.

Faith and Freedom Coalition – An advocacy organization of religious conservatives committed to educating, equipping, and mobilizing people of faith in the public square.

Federalist Society – An organization for constitutional conservative attorneys and law students.

FedUp PAC – A conservative, independent expenditure political action committee that empowers 3 million+ grassroots conservatives to act like modern-day Paul Reveres to educate 100 million+ Americans using FedUp PAC-produced "ready-to-use" voter education materials that bypass Big Media and Big Tech in the effort to create a constitutional conservative governing majority in Congress.

Fund for American Studies – Teaches principles of limited government, free-market economics, and honorable leadership to students and young professionals in America and around the world.

Heritage Action – The lobbying arm of the Heritage Foundation.

Heritage Foundation – The world's largest conservative think tank dealing with public policy.

Intercollegiate Studies Institute (ISI) – An educational organization that promotes conservative thought on college campuses.

Judicial Watch – Exposes government lawbreaking by promoting transparency, accountability and integrity in government, politics and the law, using litigation and Freedom of Information Act requests.

Leadership Institute – Provides training in campaigns, fundraising, grassroots organizing, youth politics, and communications. The Institute teaches conservatives of all ages how to succeed in politics, government, and the media.

Reagan Alumni Association – An organization of those who worked in a Reagan campaign and/or served in the Reagan administration, founded and led by Lou Cordia.

Media Research Center – A research and education organization that exposes the leftist bias of the news media and popular culture.

The Conservative Caucus – A conservative public policy and lobbying organization that emphasizes grassroots citizen activism.

Young America's Foundation (YAF) – A conservative youth organization that introduces students to conservative ideas through conferences, campus lectures, and initiatives.

Sources for Conservative News and Information

The American Conservative (TAC) – A bi-monthly magazine that promotes "Main Street" conservatism and seeks to restore constitutional conservatism.

American Spectator – Informs the public on new ideas, concepts, and policies that favor traditional American values, such as economic freedom, individual liberty, self-sufficiency, and limited government.

American Thinker – A daily online publication devoted to the thoughtful exploration of issues of importance to conservatives.

Blaze Media – A conservative source for news and entertainment, available online and on television, radio, and podcast, founded by Glenn Beck, and featuring BlazeTV.

Bott Radio Network – A network of Christian radio stations in the United States, broadcasting Christian talk and teaching programs.

Breitbart News Network – A conservative website that includes syndicated news, opinion, and commentary founded by the legendary Andrew Breitbart.

ConservativeHQ.com – News and information for conservative leaders and activists that will help grow the conservative movement so large that conservatives will soon govern America, founded by Richard A. Viguerie.

CNSNews – From Media Research Center, original reporting and breaking news.

Daily Caller – A 24-hour online news publication founded by Tucker Carlson providing original reporting, commentary, and breaking news.

Daily Wire – A conservative daily outlet that provides news, opinion, and entertainment, founded by Ben Shapiro.

Donaldjtrump.com/news – Read the latest news and analysis on President Donald Trump. Follow today's top stories and breaking news from inside Washington, D.C., and beyond.

Epoch Times – Conservative publication that reports on politics, world, business, and opinion (anti-communism especially Red China–publication by Falun Gong; available by print and online).

The Federalist – A conservative web magazine that focuses on culture, politics, and religion.

Fox News – Branded as a fair and balanced news network founded by Rupert Murdoch that provides hourly programming including Bret Baier at 6:00 pm, Jesse Watters at 7:00 pm, Tucker Carlson at 8:00 pm, and other popular right-of-center personalities.

Gateway Pundit – An online publication that provides news, commentary, and analysis.

Human Events – A conservative political news and analysis digital newspaper founded in 1944.

Imprimis – A free monthly speech digest with 6.2 million subscribers published by Hillsdale College. It is dedicated to educating citizens and promoting civil and religious liberty by covering cultural, economic, political, and educational issues. The content of *Imprimis* is drawn from speeches delivered at Hillsdale College events.

Instapundit – A libertarian, conservative blog with links to news and culture stories updated throughout the day by law professor Glenn Reynolds and various superb writers.

LifeSiteNews – Online newspaper that provides pro-life news, information, and opinion to help defend life, family, faith, and culture.

National Review – Bi-weekly conservative magazine that covers news, politics, current events, and culture with both analysis and commentary, founded by Bill Buckley, Jr.

Newsmax – A conservative monthly print news magazine, website, and cable news station founded by Chris Ruddy that features politics and opinion. The cable channel primarily carries news, talk, and opinion format programming.

PJ Media – A news website covering politics, faith, homeland security, and more.

RedState – A conservative blog and news source owned by Salem Media Group.

Salem Media Group – A radio broadcaster, internet content provider, and magazine and book publisher targeting audiences interested in Christian values, family-themed content, and conservative political issues.

Tips – A free weekly blog on marketing and fundraising by Kevin Gentry. Email kevin.gentry@kochps.com to subscribe.

Townhall.org – A part of Salem Media Group, it features top-notch breaking news reporting, political commentary, and analysis from well over 100 leading columnists and opinion leaders, conservative talk-radio, and a community of millions of grassroots conservatives.

Washington Examiner – A conservative news website and weekly magazine that provides news, opinion, and commentary.

Washington Free-Beacon – A conservative online newspaper that provides in-depth, investigative reporting on public policy, government affairs, international security, and the media.

The Washington Times – A conservative daily newspaper that delivers news and commentary on the issues that affect the future of our nation from a conservative viewpoint.

Western Journal – They aggregate news of interest to conservatives, founded by Floyd Brown.

Annual Conferences

American Legislative Exchange Council (ALEC)

Conservative Political Action Conference (CPAC) – An annual gathering for conservative activists and grassroots political activists that features many prominent public figures.

Faith and Freedom Coalition's Road to Majority

FreedomFest

Heritage Resource Bank

Media Research Center Annual Gala

Moms for America

Napa Institute

National Rifle Association Annual Meeting

SHOT Show – Open to shooting, outdoors, hunting, and law enforcement trade groups only.

State Policy Network

Turning Point USA – They have many events, including:

- Saving America Tour
- Educate Don't Mandate Tour
- Young Women's Leadership Summit
- Student Action Summit
- Pastor's Summit
- AmericaFest

Western CPAC – Like CPAC, an annual gathering of conservatives, held in the western states.

Young Americans For Freedom (YAF) – National Conservative Student Conference.

Educational Sources

Hillsdale College – A renown private liberal arts college that provides moral and social instruction as will best develop the minds and improve the hearts of its students. It specializes in teaching America's founding documents. Its publication, *Imprimis*, is a free monthly speech digest with over 6 million subscribers, dedicated to educating citizens and promoting civil and religious liberty. Hillsdale's free online courses were created for every American who wishes to embark upon a life-changing education in the greatest ideas and texts of Western Civilization.

PragerU – Promotes American values through the creative use of educational videos that reach millions of people online. Serving all ages, the content offers a free alternative to the dominant leftwing ideology in culture, media, and education. Not an accredited university by design.

Appendix 3

The Laws of the Public Policy Process

1. Never give a bureaucrat a chance to say no.
2. Don't fire all your ammunition at once.
3. Don't get mad except on purpose.
4. Effort is admirable. Achievement is valuable.
5. Make the steal more expensive than it's worth.
6. Give 'em a title and get 'em involved.
7. Expand the leadership.
8. You can't beat a plan with no plan.
9. Political technology determines political success.
10. Sound doctrine is sound politics.
11. In politics, you have your word and your friends; go back on either and you're dead.
12. Keep your eye on the main chance and don't stop to kick every barking dog.
13. Don't make the perfect the enemy of the good.
14. Remember the other side has troubles too.
15. Don't treat good guys like you treat bad guys.
16. A well-run movement takes care of its own.
17. Hire at least as many to the right of you as to the left of you.
18. You can't save the world if you can't pay the rent.
19. All gains are incremental; some increments aren't gains.
20. A stable movement requires a healthy, reciprocal IOU flow among its participants.
21. Don't keep a careful tally.
22. An ounce of loyalty is worth a pound of cleverness.

23. Never miss a political meeting if you think there's the slightest chance you'd wish you'd been there.

24. In volunteer politics, a builder can build faster than a destroyer can destroy.

25. Actions have consequences.

26. The mind can absorb no more than the seat can endure.

27. Personnel is policy.

28. Remember it's a long ball game.

29. The test of moral ideas is moral results.

30. You can't beat somebody with nobody.

31. Better a snake in the grass than a viper in your bosom.

32. Don't fully trust anyone until he has stuck with a good cause that he saw was losing.

33. A prompt, generous letter of thanks can seal a commitment that otherwise might disappear when the going gets rough.

34. Governing is campaigning by different means.

35. You cannot make friends of your enemies by making enemies of your friends.

36. Choose your enemies as carefully as you choose your friends.

37. Keep a secure home base.

38. Don't rely on being given anything you don't ask for.

39. In politics, nothing moves unless it's pushed.

40. Winners aren't perfect. They made fewer mistakes than their rivals.

41. One big reason is better than many little reasons.

42. In moments of crisis, the initiative passes to those who are best prepared.

43. Politics is of the heart as well as of the mind. Many people don't care how much you know until they know how much you care.

44. Promptly report your action to the one who requested it.
45. Moral outrage is the most powerful motivating force in politics.
46. Pray as if it all depended on God; work as if it all depended on you.

Morton C. Blackwell
President, The Leadership Institute

Appendix 4
Useful Guides

Full versions of both articles listed below can be found at www.GoBigLinks.com.

Morton Blackwell's *The Conservative Organizational Entrepreneur* https://www.leadershipinstitute.org/writings/?ID=22

> Written by Morton Blackwell as a guide for conservative organizational entrepreneurs, this book "explains how you can create an effective organization for your public policy activities." It gives the tools and advice on being a true organizational entrepreneur, organizational growth, an organization's mission, organization categories and levels to choose from, attorneys and accountants, board of directors, advisory committee, endorsers, how to plan your growth, how to fund your organization, how to make things happen, etc.

Helen Blackwell's *Crash Course in Courtesy* https://www.leadershipinstitute.org/writings/?ID=65

> This is a complete guide written by Helen Blackwell, "Mrs. Manners," on how to be a wonderful house guest. This follows decades of the Blackwells' home being used as a home for thousands of Leadership Institute students and future conservative leaders.

Appendix 5

100 Largest Right-of-Center Nonprofits
by Annual Revenues, FY 2017–2020
Prepared: April 2022

	Organization	Gross Receipts	FY
1	WinRed (2019–2020 Cycle)	$2,240,123,104	2020
2	National Christian Charitable Foundation	$2,004,332,984	2019
3	Senate Leadership Fund (PAC: 2019–2020 Cycle)	$475,355,109	2020
4	National Rifle Association*	$367,702,748	2018
5	Charles Koch Funded Organizations	$275,126,973	
6	Hillsdale College	$211,487,883	2019
7	Judicial Watch	$162,515,598	2019
8	America First Action (PAC: 2019–2020 Cycle)	$150,128,473	2020
9	Heritage Foundation	$132,836,267	2019
10	NRA Foundation	$121,196,829	2019
11	National Federation of Independent Business	$104,660,533	2019
12	Focus on the Family	$99,205,813	2019
13	*Americans for Prosperity (See #5)**	*$98,591,581*	*2018*
14	Institute for Justice	$83,969,192	2019
15	American Crossroads	$81,809,711	2019
16	Alliance Defending Freedom	$76,822,141	2019
17	Hoover Institution	$70,625,000	2020
18	National Shooting Sports Foundation	$70,395,940	2019
19	Club for Growth Action (PAC: 2019–2020 Cycle)	$66,334,260	2020
20	Foundation for Economic Education	$64,248,222	2020
21	*Charles Koch Institute (See #5)**	*$60,913,751*	*2018*

22	Hudson Institute	$60,711,844	2019
23	*Americans for Prosperity PAC (See #5)*	*$60,382,095*	*2020*
24	American Enterprise Institute	$59,701,236	2019
25	Christian Advocates Serving Evangelism	$57,497,216	2019
26	American Action Network*	$51,839,313	2018
27	Turning Point USA	$39,843,289	2020
28	Federation for American Immigration Reform	$39,441,822	2019
29	*Stand Together (See #5)**	*$37,246,447*	*2018*
30	Prager University Foundation	$36,769,692	2019
31	Young America's Foundation	$33,050,410	2019
32	CATO Institute	$32,721,086	2019
33	Foundation for the Defense of Democracies	$32,652,793	2019
34	Mercatus Center	$31,817,687	2019
35	Daughters of the American Revolution	$31,042,195	2019
36	Freedom Alliance*	$28,736,654	2018
37	Faith and Freedom Coalition*	$27,557,974	2018
38	National Right to Work Legal Defense & Education Fund*	$27,341,254	2018
39	Federalist Society for Law and Public Policy Studies*	$26,422,862	2018
40	NRA Political Victory Fund (PAC: 2019–2020 Cycle)	$23,421,777	2020
41	American Center for Law and Justice	$22,991,480	2019
42	American Family Association	$21,480,988	2019
43	Texas Public Policy Foundation	$21,300,334	2019
44	Americans for Tax Reform	$20,798,802	2019
45	State Policy Network	$20,348,540	2019
46	Manhattan Institute for Policy Research	$19,835,647	2019
47	Leadership Institute	$19,638,460	2019
48	Institute for Humane Studies*	$19,635,716	2018
49	Pacific Legal Foundation	$18,427,010	2019
50	American Future Fund*	$18,348,315	2018

51	*Americans for Prosperity Foundation (See #5)**	*$17,993,099*	*2018*
52	Family Research Council	$17,410,139	2019
53	American Conservative Union	$16,702,315	2019
54	Reason Foundation	$16,170,727	2020
55	Atlas Network	$15,289,731	2019
56	First Liberty Institute	$14,810,344	2020
57	Fund for American Studies	$14,414,710	2019
58	Media Research Center	$13,821,698	2019
59	Foundation for Individual Rights in Education	$13,740,060	2020
60	Home School Legal Defense Association	$13,359,054	2019
61	Heritage Action for America	$11,685,980	2019
62	Citizens United	$11,151,839	2019
63	Susan B. Anthony List	$11,005,738	2019
64	Priests for Life	$10,649,738	2018
65	Acton Institute for the Study of Religion and Liberty	$10,475,844	2019
66	FreedomWorks	$10,404,099	2019
67	Foundation for Government Accountability*	$9,424,541	2018
68	American Legislative Exchange Council*	$9,357,918	2018
69	National Right to Work Committee	$8,843,095	2019
70	FreedomWorks Foundation	$8,379,908	2020
71	EdChoice (Choice in Education)	$8,110,345	2020
72	Becket Fund	$7,480,239	2020
73	American Studies Center	$7,138,987	2019
74	Ayn Rand Institute	$6,986,678	2019
75	Competitive Enterprise Institute	$6,805,470	2020
76	Pacific Research Institute for Public Policy	$6,107,734	2019
77	National Association for Gun Rights	$6,093,701	2019
78	Intercollegiate Studies Institute	$6,014,026	2020
79	Gun Owners of America	$5,866,266	2019

80	Heartland Institute*	$5,848,674	2018
81	Center for Security Policy	$5,159,496	2019
82	Capital Research Center	$4,627,330	2019
83	Second Amendment Foundation	$4,487,488	2019
84	Concerned Women for America	$4,349,197	2020
85	NumbersUSA Education and Research Foundation	$4,228,694	2019
86	Catholic Vote/Fidelis	$4,102,423	2019
87	Susan B. Anthony List Education Fund	$3,989,568	2019
88	Citizens United Foundation	$3,925,813	2019
89	National Right to Life Committee	$3,862,651	2020
90	Independent Women's Forum	$3,751,181	2019
91	American Life League	$3,632,583	2019
92	John Locke Foundation	$3,413,515	2020
93	60 Plus Association*	$3,390,070	2018
94	Council for National Policy	$3,310,081	2019
95	Center for Immigration Studies	$3,244,681	2019
96	Americans United for Life	$3,200,917	2019
97	Ethics and Public Policy Center	$3,097,891	2019
98	Citizens Against Government Waste	$2,764,560	2019
99	AMAC Action	$2,424,056	2020
100	Thomas B. Fordham Institute	$2,169,138	2019
		$8,078,932,107	

* Indicates 2017 or 2018 numbers, which are the most current 990s posted online as of January 28, 2022.

- WinRed is a GOP for-profit fundraising platform endorsed by the Republican National Committee to help elect Republican candidates. It was launched to compete with the Democratic Party's success in online grassroots fundraising with their platform, ActBlue.
- We are using annual budget numbers (Gross Receipts)

based on 2017–2020 totals, whichever is the most current number available.

- Sources: www.projects.propublica.org/nonprofits, opensecrets.org, guidestar.org and sourcewatch.org.
- Of the ideological organizations with annual budgets over $100 million, liberals have 33 and conservatives have 10.
- Of the ideological organizations with annual budgets of $1 billion or more, liberals have 6 while conservatives only have 2.
- Liberals have about 20,000 nonprofit organizations. Conservatives have about 1,000–2,000. In recent years, the Left raised 700% more money from their nonprofit organizations from about 700% more donors.

There is no exact science in selecting the organizations on this list. Reasonable people may disagree on whether any particular organization should be listed or not, but we used our best judgement as well as outside experts to compile this list. This fact is clear: liberal nonprofit organizations are massively outraising conservative organizations.

Appendix 6

100 Largest Left-of-Center/Progressive Nonprofits
by Annual Revenues, FY 2017-2020
Prepared: April 2022

	Organization	Gross Receipts	FY
1	AARP	$27,828,138,657	2019
2	ActBlue (PAC: 2019–2020 Cycle)	$4,318,377,981	2020
3	Nature Conservancy*	$2,096,240,637	2018
4	National Association of Letter Carriers	$2,046,526,116	2019
5	Planned Parenthood & Affiliates	$1,641,400,000	2019
6	AARP Foundation	$966,873,763	2019
7	Arabella Advisors Network	$845,285,256	
8	Tides Funded Operations	$844,262,673	
9	*Tides Foundation (See #8)*	*$564,636,182*	*2019*
10	*New Venture Fund (See #7)*	*$497,977,645*	*2019*
11	World Wildlife Fund	$317,026,832	2019
12	Service Employees International Union	$299,368,207	2019
13	American Civil Liberties Union	$295,735,238	2020
14	Natural Resources Defense Council	$262,737,928	2020
15	Educational Media Foundation	$231,043,542	2019
16	American Federation of Teachers	$216,471,260	2019
17	Environmental Defense Fund	$209,482,487	2019
18	Sierra Club Foundation	$203,051,929	2020
19	*Tides Center (See #8)*	*$201,105,395*	*2019*
20	Council on Foreign Relations	$188,420,600	2020
21	Communications Workers of America	$185,200,723	2019
22	Sierra Club	$178,289,421	2019
23	Barack Obama Foundation	$162,526,720	2019
24	AFSCME*	$161,912,610	2017
25	Trust for Public Lands	$161,225,350	2019
26	*Hopewell Fund (See #7)*	*$159,029,026*	*2019*

27	Brookings Institution	$151,692,796	2019
28	*Sixty Thirty Fund (See #7)*	*$143,873,877*	*2019*
29	Priorities USA Action (PAC: 2019–2020 Cycle)	$139,463,406	2020
30	Pathfinder International	$138,012,335	2019
31	Human Rights Watch	$125,594,780	2019
32	Southern Poverty Law Center	$118,765,026	2019
33	NEO Philanthropy	$106,981,767	2019
34	Bill, Hillary, and Chelsea Clinton Foundation	$100,356,699	2019
35	National Wildlife Federation	$94,376,443	2019
36	ClimateWorks Foundation	$93,577,498	2019
37	Black Lives Matter Global Network Foundation	$90,000,000	2020
38	American Federation of Government Employees*	$88,966,134	2018
39	Everytown for Gun Safety Action Fund	$84,791,737	2019
40	American Bridge 21st Century**	$81,588,769	2018
41	Democracy PAC (PAC: 2019–2020 Cycle)	$81,378,923	2020
42	Emily's List (PAC: 2019–2020 Cycle)	$77,826,316	2020
43	AFL-CIO**	$75,965,111	2018
44	Progressive Turnout PAC (PAC: 2019–2020 Cycle)	$74,555,908	2020
45	National Urban League	$72,627,495	2019
46	People for the Ethical Treatment of Animals	$69,319,713	2020
47	North Fund	$66,608,974	2019
48	League of Conservation Voters**	$65,184,681	2018
49	Entertainment Industry Foundation	$59,290,881	2019
50	Task Force for Global Health	$56,376,601	2019
51	*Tides Advocacy (See #8)*	*$55,015,332*	*2019*
52	Center for American Progress	$48,041,725	2019
53	PEW Research Center	$46,814,888	2019
54	Human Rights Campaign (homosexual issues)	$44,604,113	2020
55	*Windward Fund (See #7)*	*$44,404,708*	*2019*
56	Voter Registration Project	$43,767,638	2019
57	Greenpeace	$36,732,324	2019
58	Everytown for Gun Safety Support Fund	$34,097,970	2019

59	Director's Guild of America	$33,853,278	2019
60	Proteus Fund	$30,644,661	2019
61	America Votes	$29,660,265	2019
62	Center for Popular Democracy	$28,906,156	2019
63	Guttmacher Institute (abortion issues)	$24,255,758	2019
64	*Tides Network (See #8)*	*$23,505,764*	*2019*
65	Greenpeace Fund	$19,972,484	2019
66	Friends of the Earth	$19,801,719	2019
67	Human Rights Campaign Foundation	$15,135,399	2020
68	Media Matters for America	$14,556,285	2019
69	NEO Philanthropy Action Fund	$13,226,182	2019
70	Feminist Majority Foundation	$12,379,635	2019
71	NARAL Pro-Choice America	$12,244,707	2019
72	Race Forward	$11,012,148	2019
73	Western Resource Advocates	$10,157,957	2019
74	Institute for Sustainable Communities	$9,579,944	2019
75	Brady Center to Prevent Gun Violence	$8,606,061	2019
76	Equality Now	$7,930,087	2019
77	Urgent Action Fund for Women's Human Rights	$7,894,744	2019
78	Center for Environmental Health	$7,716,568	2019
79	Alliance for Global Justice	$6,977,638	2020
80	National Day Laborer Organizing Network	$6,607,618	2019
81	PFLAG (homosexual issues)	$5,753,391	2020
82	Environmental Integrity Project	$5,555,302	2019
83	Planned Parenthood Center for Choice	$5,465,105	2019
84	CarbonFund.org Foundation	$5,373,825	2019
85	Southern Alliance for Clean Energy*	$5,024,926	2018
86	ColorofChange.org	$5,018,183	2019
87	Earthworks	$4,597,756	2020
88	Western Center on Law & Poverty	$4,471,606	2019
89	Center for International Environmental Law	$4,385,045	2020
90	National Organization for Women	$4,351,612	2019
91	Center for Economic Research	$4,333,658	2019
92	Center for Climate and Energy Solutions	$4,260,983	2019
93	Clean Air Council*	$4,185,567	2017

94	GLBTQ Legal Advocates and Defenders	$4,132,941	2020
95	Alliance for Climate Education	$4,015,247	2020
96	National Center for Transgender Equality	$3,749,947	2019
97	Earthcorps	$3,621,142	2019
98	Oil Change International	$3,522,810	2020
99	Partnership for a New American Economy Action Fund*	$3,344,984	2018
100	American Council for Renewable Energy	$3,203,539	2019
	TOTAL	$46,446,445,444	

* Indicates 2017 or 2018 numbers, which are the most current 990s posted online as of January 28, 2022.

** Budget numbers taken from 2018 Annual Report.

- We are using annual budget numbers (Gross Receipts) based on 2017–2020 totals, whichever is the most current number available.
- Sources: www.projects.propublica.org/nonprofits, opensecrets.org, guidestar.org and sourcewatch.org.
- Of the ideological organizations with annual budgets over $100 million, liberals have 33 and conservatives have 10.
- Of the ideological organizations with annual budgets of $1 billion or more, liberals have 6 while conservatives only have 2.
- Liberals have about 20,000 nonprofit organizations. Conservatives have about 1,000–2,000. In recent years, the Left raised 700% more money from their nonprofit organizations from about 700% more donors.

There is no exact science in selecting the organizations on this list. Reasonable people may disagree on whether any particular organization should be listed or not, but we used our best judgement as well as outside experts to compile this list. This fact is clear: liberal nonprofit organizations are massively outraising conservative organizations.

Appendix 7

20 Largest Private Conservative
Family Foundations (FY 2019)
Prepared: April 2022

	Foundation	Assets 2019
1	Andrew W. Mellon Foundation	$6,993,000,000
2	John Templeton Foundation	$3,329,000,000
3	Anschutz Foundation	$1,497,659,862
4	Lynde & Harry Bradley Foundation	$934,410,986
5	Paul E. Singer Foundation	$805,439,112
6	Sarah Scaife Foundation	$870,946,716
7	Smith Richardson Family Foundation	$469,899,873
8	Adolph Coors Foundation	$205,606,623
9	Donors Trust	$216,035,758
10	Heavenly Father's Foundation (Dan & Staci Wilks)	$193,039,818
11	William H. Donner Foundation	$192,902,150
12	Gleason Family Foundation	$168,628,312
13	Dick and Betsy DeVos Family Foundation	$65,094,061
14	Stephen A. Schwarzman Foundation	$60,764,688
15	Randolph Foundation	$51,988,072
16	Hickory Foundation	$37,531,837
17	Thomas A. Roe Foundation	$28,134,334
18	Ed Uihlein Family Foundation	$24,772,594
19	Philip M. McKenna Foundation	$18,543,400
20	Claws Foundation (Jeffery Yass)	$10,591,987
	TOTAL	$16,173,990,183

You will note that the twentieth-largest liberal foundation has assets of over $2 billion vs. $10 million for the twentieth-largest conservative foundation.

Appendix 8

20 Largest Private Liberal Family Foundations (FY 2019)
Prepared: April 2022

	Foundation	Assets 2019
1	Bill & Melinda Gates Foundation	$51,038,075,591
2	Ford Foundation	$14,230,472,678
3	Robert Wood Johnson Foundation	$11,911,586,700
4	William and Flora Hewlett Foundation	$10,961,138,137
5	Foundation to Promote Open Society (George Soros)	$10,603,152,570
6	Bloomberg Family Foundation	$8,651,356,138
7	David and Lucile Packard Foundation	$7,969,450,311
8	John and Catherine MacArthur Foundation	$7,208,352,632
9	Gordon and Betty Moore Foundation	$7,171,712,288
10	Rockefeller Foundation	$4,929,907,452
11	Conrad N. Hilton Foundation	$4,101,713,350
12	Kresge Foundation	$3,838,563,502
13	California Endowment	$3,477,908,960
14	Open Society Institute (George Soros)	$3,477,908,960
15	Carnegie Corporation of New York	$3,444,166,743
16	JPB Foundation (formerly Picower Foundation)	$3,264,553,827
17	Charles Stewart Mott Foundation	$3,194,986,402
18	William Penn Foundation	$2,825,827,362
19	Susan Thompson Buffett Foundation	$2,084,499,584
20	Annie E. Casey Foundation	$2,002,659,666
	TOTAL	$166,387,992,853

You will note that the twentieth-largest liberal foundation has assets of over $2 billion vs. $10 million for the twentieth-largest conservative foundation.

There is no exact science in selecting the organizations on this list. Reasonable people may disagree on whether any particular organization should be listed or not, but we used our best judgement as well as outside experts to compile this list. This fact is clear: liberal nonprofit organizations are massively outraising conservative organizations.

Appendix 9

Photographs

Lee Edwards, Phyllis Schlafly, and Richard Viguerie (pictured left to right) at a conservative gathering in 2013.

Paul and Joyce Weyrich, Elaine and Richard Viguerie, and Senator Paul and Mrs. Carol Laxalt (pictured left to right), at a victory dinner honoring Senator Laxalt and Viguerie for their leadership that led to the defeat of President Jimmy Carter's 1977 attempt to change election laws in favor of the Democrats.

Ronald Reagan and Richard Viguerie peruse copies of
Conservative Digest in the spring of 1975.

Lee Edwards, Richard Viguerie, and Lou Cordia
at a conservative event in 2022.

Appendix 10
Podcasts and Videos

Podcast with national marketer Joe Polish re: Four
Horsemen & The Four-Part Plan that Leads to Success
(www.GoBigLinks.com)

> *In this audio, Viguerie gives an overview of his Four
> Horsemen of Marketing®, as well as Newt's Four-Part Plan.
> He also discusses how to market using postal mail and the
> internet.*

Podcast with Joe Polish re: Four Horsemen of Marketing®
(www.GoBigLinks.com)

> *In this audio, Viguerie elaborates on his Four Horsemen of
> Marketing® and how it relates to his success and the success
> of others. He also gives an insight to his values, views, and
> even health habits for a productive and happy life.*

Richard Viguerie discussing the Four Horsemen
(www.GoBigLinks.com)

> *In this video, you'll learn the importance of unique ability,
> the Four Horsemen of Marketing®, and the nine critical ways
> to market successfully through snail mail.*

Appendix 11

Books by Richard A. Viguerie

- *The New Right, We're Ready to Lead* (1981)
- *The Establishment vs. the People* (1983) – Is a New Populist Revolt on the Way?
- *America's Right Turn* (2004) – How Conservatives Used New and Alternative Media to Take Power.
- *Conservatives Betrayed* (2006) – How George W. Bush and Other Big Government Republicans Hijacked the Conservative Cause.
- *How Conservatives Can Outlive Liberals* (2013) – Richard Viguerie explains why at age 89 he's able to work 12–13 hours a day, five and a half days a week.
- *TAKEOVER* (2014) – The 100-Year War for the Soul of the GOP and How Conservatives Can Finally Win It.

Appendix 12
Viguerieisms
Classic Sayings of "002"

1. The purpose of our company is to save America and Western Civilization.
2. It didn't happen today, but I promise you, tomorrow before the sun sets, I will save America and Western Civilization. (As I've been saying for over 60 years.)
3. Direct Mail is the easiest way I know to make a living.
4. I wouldn't dream of flying in an airplane with a pilot who had the pilot skills of the average person in direct marketing.
5. Everyone needs mentors and coaches.
6. Who's your mentor/coach?
7. What's your hole in the marketplace?
8. It's easy to get out of line, but almost impossible to cut into line (meaning, reserve your print time, lettershop time, and list reservations now, etc.)
9. Let's blow and go (meaning, let's move quickly and boldly).
10. This reads like you parachuted into the person's life.
11. Is this statement true?
12. This is a cuss package—it just cusses the problem.
13. The donor is smarter than you. They have the money, and you don't.
14. Never underestimate the intelligence of your reader.
15. Don't keep it a secret!
16. What direct mail/marketing books are you reading?
17. What's the last marketing book you read?
18. Study, Study, Read, Read the giants in direct mail/marketing/communications.

19. What's the bottom line? (An entrepreneur will always look for the bottom line. Have you totaled your column of numbers?)
20. This package is too "thin."
21. What's the downside? I know the upside.
22. This package won't be successful—it doesn't lead with a technique.
23. This is not a serious survey/poll written for a serious person.
24. Paint a picture with your copy.
25. If it's not in the conservative media, we can't raise money on the issue.
26. Write for the ages.
27. Think and act like an entrepreneur.
28. Let's gut rollout (mail a large amount of letters without testing).
29. Write a serious letter about a serious problem, proposing a serious solution to a friend.
30. Republicans never win elections unless they're nationalized around conservative issues.
31. It's the primaries, stupid!
32. We conservatives should operate as a third force independent of the Democrats and establishment Republicans, pulling all to the right.
33. Conservatives must not operate as an appendage/arm of the GOP.
34. It's easier to grow 1,000% than 100% (Dan Sullivan, Strategic Coach).
35. Say "Thank You" and say it often.
36. ATA is not as much a marketing agency as a university—as a high percent of our "competitors" are former ATA executives. That's good, because most all are advancing the conservative cause.

37. You can do most anything.
    You just have to do one thing.
    You don't have to like doing it.
    You don't have to agree that you have to do this.
    You don't have to believe you have to do it.
    But you **HAVE** to do this one thing.
    PAY THE PRICE.

Index

10× thinking 36, 139–44, 148
60 Plus Association 177
501(c)(3)s *xiii*, 103, 135–36
501(c)(4)s 135
700 Club 76–77

AARP 179
ABC 14, 19, 60, 96
abortion 31, 38, 41, 54, 68, 151, 181
ActBlue 5, 53, 177, 179
Acton Institute for the Study of Religion and Liberty 176
Adolph Coors Foundation 183
Advancing American Freedom 163
AFL-CIO 107, 180
The Agitator 162
Ahern, Tom 87, 162
Alliance Defending Freedom 77, 163, 174
Alliance for Climate Education 182
Alliance for Global Justice 181
Alliance for Justice 135
AMAC Action 177
Amazon 142
America First Action 174
America First Policy Institute 163
American Action Network 175
American Airlines 17
American Bridge 21st Century 180
American Center for Law and Justice 175
American Civil Liberties Union (ACLU) 5, 179
The American Conservative (TAC) 165
American Conservative Union (ACU) *viii*, 76, 113, 163, 176
American Council for Renewable Energy 182
American Crossroads 174
American Enterprise Institute *xii*, 175
American Family Association 175
American Federation of Government Employees 180
American Federation of State, County and Municipal Employees (AFSCME) 179
American Federation of Teachers 179
American Future Fund 175
American Legislative Exchange Council 168, 176

American Legislative Exchange Council (ALEC) 168
American Life League 177
American Security Council 76
Americans for Constitutional Action (ACA) 8
Americans for Prosperity 174, 175, 176
Americans for Prosperity Foundation 176
Americans for Tax Reform 175
American Spectator 165
American Studies Center 176
Americans United for Life 76, 177
American Target Advertising (ATA) *iv*, *xv*, 1, 50, 55, 89, 112, 123, 132, 139, 143–50, 160–61, 193
American Thinker 165
America Votes 181
Andrew W. Mellon Foundation 183
Annie E. Casey Foundation 184
Anschutz Foundation 183
Arabella Advisors Network 179
Armstrong, Richard *ix*
Arnn, Larry 77, 142
Associated Press 27
Association of Community Organizations for Reform Now (ACORN) 70
Atlas Network 176
Ayers, Bill 134
Ayn Rand Institute 176

Baier, Bret 14, 166
Baker, Howard 73, 76
Bakersmith, Nancy 160
Baltimore Sun x
Barack Obama Foundation 179
Barkan, Ady 26
Barrett, Amy Coney 62
Barton, Bruce 162
Bauman, Robert 10
Becket Fund 176
Beck, Glenn 14, 165
Bennett, Joan 160
Benson, Richard V. (Dick) 13, 81, 162
Bezos, Jeff 52, 78, 155
Biden, Hunter 93
Biden, Joe 24, 26–27, 54, 58, 67, 71, 93, 157
Big Media 2, 25, 62, 92–93, 105, 117, 151, 164

Big Tech 2, 25, 31, 52, 62, 92–93, 117, 151, 153, 164
Bill, Hillary, and Chelsea Clinton Foundation 180
Bill & Melinda Gates Foundation 184
Black Lives Matter Global Network Foundation 180
Blackwell, Helen *xiv, xv*
Blackwell, Morton *vii, xii–xv*, 33, 35, 63, 77, 119, 172–73
Blaze Media 165
Bloomberg Family Foundation 184
Bloomberg, Mike 52, 78, 155, 184
Boehner, John 73
Bolder Advocacy 135
Bott Radio Network 165
Bozell, Brent, Jr. 11
Bradbury, Dottie 160
Bradley, Lynde & Harry 183
Brady Center to Prevent Gun Violence 181
Breitbart, Andrew 165
Breitbart News Network 165
Brock, Bill 108–9
Broder, David *x*
Brookings Institution 180
Brown, Floyd 168
Buckley, Patricia 8
Buckley, Priscilla 11
Buckley, William F., Jr. 8–9, 11, 56, 75, 167
Buffett, Susan Thompson 184
Burke, Edmund 11
Burnett, Ken 162
Burnett, Leo 115
Burnham, James 11
Bush, Cori 27
Bush, George H. W. 66, 76
Bush, George W. 70, 191
Bush, Jeb 18
Byrd, Bobby 111

California Endowment 184
Campaigne, Jameson 161
campaign financing 111, 134
cancel culture 100, 117, 149
Capital Research Center 163, 177
Caples, John 13, 81
Caray, Harry 7
CarbonFund.org 181
Carlson, Tucker 14, 56, 58, 64, 95, 108, 166
Carnegie Corporation of New York 184
cars (auto safety) 79
Carter, Jimmy 110, 111–12, 187
Carville, James 66
Casey, Annie E. 184

Catastrophic Health Act 112
Catholicism 31, 41
CatholicVote 163
Catholic Vote/Fidelis 177
CATO Institute 175
CBS 14, 19, 60, 96
Center for American Progress 180
Center for Climate and Energy Solutions 181
Center for Economic Research 181
Center for Environmental Health 181
Center for Immigration Studies 177
Center for International Environmental Law 181
Center for Popular Democracy 181
Center for Security Policy 177
Central Intelligence Agency (CIA) 2, 151
Chambers, Whitaker 11
Charles Koch Institute 174
Charles Stewart Mott Foundation 184
charter schools 30
China 8, 39, 149, 158, 166
Christianity 40, 76, 161, 165, 167, 174–75
Christie, Chris 18
The Christophers (charity) 1
Churchill, Winston 37
Cialdini, Robert B. 13, 162
Citizens Against Government Waste 177
Citizens United 176–77
Claws Foundation 183
Clean Air Council 181
climate issues 41
ClimateWorks Foundation 180
Clinton, Bill 113–14
Clinton, Hillary 33, 42, 63, 100, 113–14, 180
Club for Growth Action 174
Clymer, Adam 113
CNN 14, 19, 26, 58, 60
CNSNews 166
Cockburn, Alexander *viii*
Colbert, Stephen 27
Cole, Meredith 160
College Young Republicans *xii*
ColorofChange.org 181
Common Cause 111
common-situs picketing 100, 107–8
Communications Workers of America 179
communism *xiv*, 1–2, 7–10, 36, 70, 79, 151, 158, 166
Competitive Enterprise Institute 176
Concerned Women for America 177
The Congressional Club 76, 105, 107
Connelly, John 76
Conrad N. Hilton Foundation 184

Conservative Digest 35, 76, 188
ConservativeHQ.com 166, 203–4
Conservative Political Action Conference (CPAC) *viii*, 163, 168–69
The Constitution 40, 44, 64, 73, 92, 110, 142, 161
Cooper, Anderson 58
Coors, Adolph, Jr. 183
Cordia, Lou 165, 189
Cornyn, John 67, 73
Cortopassi, Dino 34
Council for National Policy 177
Council on Foreign Relations 179
COVID-19 27, 44, 62, 64, 68, 82
Crane, Arlene 105
Crane, Phil 104
Craver, Roger 46
crime 22, 24, 26–28, 30, 40–41, 44, 48, 57, 59, 62, 64, 102
Critical Race Theory (CRT) 22, 28, 30, 42, 57, 59, 62, 79, 93, 136
Cruz, Ted 87, 203
Cuccinelli, Ken *viii*
"cuss" letters 50, 129, 192

Daily Caller 166
Daily Wire 166
Dannemeyer, Bill 33
Dartmouth College 115
Daub, Hal 33
Daughters of the American Revolution 175
David and Lucile Packard Foundation 184
Declaration of Independence 3
Delta Airlines 17
Democracy PAC 180
Department of Agriculture 92
DeSantis, Ron 87, 203
DeVos, Betsy 183
DeVos, Dick 183
Diamandis, Peter 142
Dick and Betsy DeVos Family Foundation 183
Dingman, Dick 111
Direct Magazine x
Director's Guild of America 181
Dohrn, Bernardine 134
Dolan, Terry 33, 35
Dole, Bob 73, 76, 113
Donner, William H. 183
Donors Trust 183
Dornan, Robert 111
Drucker, Peter 34
Dunlop, John 108

Eagle Forum *xiv*, 76
Earthcorps 182
Earthworks 181
EdChoice 176
Edison, Charles 10
Edison, Thomas 10
Educational Media Foundation 179
Ed Uihlein Family Foundation 183
Edwards, Lee *vii*, *xii*, 145, 186, 189
Eisenhower, Dwight D. 7, 69
Ekanger, Dara 161
election laws 28, 65, 110, 112, 187
Ellis, Tom 35, 105–6
Emily's List 180
Employer Identification Number (EIN) 133
Entertainment Industry Foundation 180
Environmental Defense Fund 179
Environmental Integrity Project 181
Epoch Times 96, 156, 166
Equality Now 181
Equal Rights Amendment (ERA) 100
Ethics and Public Policy Center 177
European Union 158
evangelicals 31, 41
Evans, Stan 11
Everytown for Gun Safety Action Fund 180
Everytown for Gun Safety Support Fund 180
evil 7, 28, 44, 94, 99, 123

Facebook 25, 59–60, 63, 74, 86, 92, 156
Faith and Freedom Coalition 77, 164, 168, 175
Falwell, Jerry 35–36, 76
Family Research Council 176
Farris, Michael 77
Federal Bureau of Investigations (FBI) 2, 151
Federal Election Commission (FEC) 132, 134
The Federalist 164, 166, 175
Federalist Society 164, 175
Federation for American Immigration Reform 175
FedUp PAC 164
Feminist Majority Foundation 181
Feulner, Ed 33, 35, 77, 114–15, 127
Fialka, John *x*
filibusters 111
Filka, John 34
Fiorina, Carly 18
First Amendment 149
First Liberty Institute 176
Fish, Hamilton IV 103
Fitton, Tom 77, 114
Fitzgibbons, Mark *xvii*, 132–33, 146, 160

Flynn, John T. 7
Focus on the Family 174
Fogarty, Christy 46
Ford Foundation 184
Ford, Gerald 76, 106–8, 110
Fordham, Thomas B. 177
Ford Motor Company 146
Fortune 500 52
fossil fuels 28, 157
Foundation for Economic Education 174
Foundation for Government Accountability 176
Foundation for Individual Rights in Education 176
Foundation for the Defense of Democracies 175
Foundation to Promote Open Society 184
founders 1, 45, 71
Four Horsemen of Marketing *iv*, 13–15, 20, 22, 85, 190
Fox Corporation 13
Fox News 14, 19, 56, 58, 95, 117, 166
Franke, David 8–9, 12, 162
Franklin, Benjamin *v*, 78
Freedom Alliance 175
FreedomFest 114, 168
Freedom of Information Act 164
FreedomWorks 176
Friends of the Earth 181
Frist, Bill 73
Fund for American Studies 164, 176
fundraising *viii*, 11, 18, 43, 46, 49, 53, 63, 82, 87, 89, 101, 109, 122–24, 126–29, 136, 154, 162, 164, 167, 177

gasoline 28, 57, 157
Gates, Bill 52, 78, 155, 184
Gates, Melinda 184
Gateway Pundit 166
gender issues 29–30, 57, 65, 80, 146
Gentry, Kevin 1, 34, 48, 161–62, 167
George Magazine ix
get out the vote (GOTV) 136
Gingrich, Newt *vii*, 33–34, 63, 86, 100, 129, 190
GLBTQ Legal Advocates and Defenders 182
Gleason Family Foundation 183
Godin, Seth 13–14, 162
Godwin, Ron 33
Goldwater, Barry, Jr. *vii*, *xii*, 11, 35, 42, 56–57, 62, 69, 75, 101–2, 145
Gong, Falun 166
Google 25, 92
Gordon and Betty Moore Foundation 184

Gorsuch, Neil 62
Greenpeace 180–81
Greenpeace Fund 181
Gun Owners of America 76, 102, 176
guns 30, 39, 44, 69, 76, 98, 102, 176, 180–81
Guttmacher Institute 54, 181

Halbert, Gary 50
Hall, Linda 160
Hannity, Sean 14, 64
Hardy, Ben 141, 143
Harris, Kamala 26
Hart, Benjamin 162
Harvard University 9, 11
Harvey, Paul 103
Hastert, Dennis 73
Hatch Act 110–11
Heartland Institute 177
Heavenly Father's Foundation 183
Helms, Jesse 35, 76, 105–7
Heritage Foundation *vii*, *xiv*, 26, 41, 46, 51, 56, 60, 77, 115, 127–28, 145, 164, 168, 174, 176
Hewlett, Flora 184
Hewlett, William 184
Hickory Foundation 183
Hillsdale College *xiii*, 59, 77, 97, 104, 142, 166–67, 169, 174
Hilton, Conrad N. 184
Hispanics 31, 40
Hoke, Pete 12, 81
Hollywood 2, 52
Home School Legal Defense Association 77, 176
Hoover Institution 174
Hopewell Fund 179
Hopkins, Claude C. 13, 162
Houston, Sam 9
Hudson Institute 175
Human Events 35, 166
Human Rights Campaign 180–81
Human Rights Watch 180
Hume, Brit 14
Humphrey, Gordon *xii*, 69, 106

immigration 24, 27, 29, 31, 39–40, 44, 48, 57, 59, 62, 64, 93, 95, 149
Imprimis 59, 97, 156, 166–67, 169
Independent Women's Forum 177
inflation 28–29, 48, 57, 65
Ingraham, Laura 14, 56, 95
Instapundit 167
Institute for Humane Studies 175
Institute for Justice 174

Institute for Sustainable Communities 181

Intercollegiate Studies Institute 164, 176

Intercollegiate Studies Institute (ISI) 164

Internal Revenue Service (IRS) 2, 133, 135–38, 151

Islam 158

Jaffa, Harry *v*

James Madison University *xv*

Jayme, Bill 81

Jefferson, Thomas 3

Jindal, Bobby 18

John and Catherine MacArthur Foundation 184

John Locke Foundation 177

Johnson, Lyndon B. 7, 11, 56, 75

Johnson, Robert Wood, II 184

John Templeton Foundation 183

Jones, David 11

Jordan, Jim 87

JPB Foundation 184

Judaism 40, 161

Judicial Watch 56, 77, 114, 164, 174

Justice Department 2, 151

Kasich, John 18

Kavanaugh, Brett 62

Keene, David *viii*

Kelly, Megyn 14

Kemp, Jack 18

Kennedy, Edward (Teddy) 111

Kennedy, John F., Jr. *ix*

Keystone pipeline 28

Klayman, Larry 114

Koch, Charles 174

Kresge Foundation 184

Kristol, Bill 113

Kurtz, Brian 81, 162

Labor Department 107–8

LaPierre, Wayne 77

Larson, Reed 103, 107

Laxalt, Paul 35, 108–9, 111–12, 187

Leadership Institute (LI) *vii, xii–xv*, 77, 133, 164, 172–73, 175

League of Conservation Voters 180

Leary, Timothy 102

Lee, Barbara 27

Legal Services Corp. 70

LegalZoom 135

Leo Burnett Advertising Agency 115

Levin, Mark 56, 64, 87, 95

Lewis, Fulton Jr. 7

LGBTQ issues 29, 39, 57, 59, 65, 70, 93, 151, 180–81

Liddy, G. Gordon 102–3

Liebman, Marvin 8–10

LifeSiteNews 167

lifetime value (LTV) 88, 125–26, 128

Limbaugh, Rush *ix*, 7, 117, 127

Locke, John 177

Loeffler, Ted 102

Longfellow, Henry Wadsworth 152

Lott, Trent 73

Lynde & Harry Bradley Foundation 183

MacArthur, Catherine 184

MacArthur, John 184

Macy, Tim 102

Manhattan Institute for Policy Research 175

Marshall, Perry 141

Martin, Jim *ix*

Marxism 1–3, 24–26, 28, 31–32, 44–45, 50, 57, 59, 64, 73, 92–94, 97–98, 121, 147, 151, 158

Mayer, Ed Jr. 13, 81

McAuliffe, Terry 80

McCain, John 73

McCarthy, Kevin 67, 73, 203

McConnell, Mitch 67, 73, 204

McDonald, George 103

McIntyre, Thomas J. 69, 106

McKenna, Philip M. 183

Meany, George 107

Media Matters for America 181

Media Research Center 165, 166, 168, 176

Mellon, Andrew W. 183

Mercatus Center 175

Mexico 9

Meyer, Frank 11

the military 2, 40, 61, 151, 163

millennials 31

Miller, Dorothy 146

Mix, Mark 104

Moms for America 168

Moore, Betty 184

Moore, Gordon 184

Moral Majority 33, 76

Moreell, Ben 8

Mott, Charles Stewart 184

MSNBC 14, 26, 58, 60

Murdoch, Rupert 13–14, 166

Musk, Elon 87

Muth, Chuck *viii*

Napa Institute 168

NARAL Pro-Choice America 54, 181

National Association for Gun Rights 176
National Association of Letter Carriers 179
National Center for Transgender Equality 182
National Committee For An Effective Congress 111
National Committee to Preserve and Protect Medicare 113
National Congressional Club 76, 105
The National Congressional Club 105
National Conservative Political Action Committee (NCPAC) 76
National Day Laborer Organizing Network 181
national defense 62, 67, 70
National Federation of Independent Business 174
National Guard 7
National Organization for Women 181
National Public Radio (NPR) 70
National Review 8, 35, 75–76, 167
National Rifle Association (NRA) *viii*, 44, 77, 168, 174–75
National Right to Life Committee 177
National Right to Work Committee 107–8, 176
National Right to Work Foundation 76
National Right to Work Legal Defense & Education Fund 175
National Right to Work Legal Defense Foundation 103–4
National Shooting Sports Foundation 174
National Tax Limitation Committee 76
National Urban League 180
National Wildlife Federation 180
Natural Resources Defense Council 179
Nature Conservancy 179
NBC 14, 19, 27, 60, 96
NEO Philanthropy 180–81
Netanyahu, Benjamin 19
Newport, Cal 141
Newsmax 26, 56, 95, 167
New Venture Fund 179
New York Times *viii*, *x*, 9, 59–60, 96, 108, 112–13
New York Times Magazine *x*
Nixon, Richard 104
Nofziger, Lyn 76
North Fund 180
NowThis News 26
NumbersUSA Education and Research Foundation 177

Obama, Barack 5, 41, 114, 128, 134, 179

ObamaCare (Affordable Care Act) 63
Oil Change International 182
oil drilling 28, 57
Oliver, Dan 161
OneAmerica 95
O'Neill, Tip 61
Open Society Institute 184
O'Reilly, Bill 14
Overman, Eric 162

Pacific Legal Foundation 175
Pacific Research Institute for Public Policy 176
Packard, David 184
Packard, Lucile 184
Paine, Thomas 152
parents (of school children) 49, 71–72, 79–80, 96, 136
Pareto Principle 141
Parler 94
Partnership for a New American Economy Action Fund 182
Pathfinder International 180
Patrick Henry College 77
Patten, Kathleen 1, 20, 139, 146, 160
Patterson, Jerry *x*
Paul, Carol 109
Paul E. Singer Foundation 183
Paul, Ron 109
Pelosi, Nancy 24, 26, 67, 71, 203
Pence, Mike 163, 203
Penn, William 184
People for the Ethical Treatment of Animals 180
Perry, Rick 18
Pew, J. Howard 10
PEW Research Center 180
PFLAG 181
Philip M. McKenna Foundation 183
Phillips, Howard 33, 35, 68–69
Phillips, Tom 115–16
Picower Foundation 184
PJ Media 167
Planned Parenthood 4, 54, 68, 70, 179, 181
police 24, 26–27, 30, 40, 48, 57, 59, 62, 64, 79, 86, 93, 95, 149
Poliengine.com 66
Political Action Committee (PAC) 135–36, 164, 174–75, 179–80
politically correct 32
Politico 5
poverty 130
Prager, Dennis 95, 175
PragerU 169

Priests for Life 138, 176
Princeton University 9, 11
Priorities USA Action 180
privacy 31
Progressive Turnout PAC 180
progressivism 1, 24–25, 31, 59, 69, 79, 92–94, 97–98, 121
Proteus Fund 181
Putin, Vladimir 28

Race Forward 181
racism 28, 30, 65, 79, 151
Rand, Ayn 176
Randolph Foundation 183
Reagan, Ronald *ix–x, xii, xiv,* 25, 35–36, 56, 59, 62, 71, 76, 100–101, 106–9, 112, 153–54, 161, 165, 188
Reason Foundation 176
RedState 167
Reed, Ralph 77
Reeves, Rosser 13, 81
religion 2, 31, 151, 166
religious freedom *xiii,* 38, 44, 59, 68, 94, 134, 155, 157
Reporter of Direct Mail 12
Revere, Paul 25, 31, 59, 64, 97–98, 152–53, 158, 164, 205
Reynolds, Glenn 167
Rhatican, Bill 110
Richardson, H. L. (Bill) 102
Richardson, H. Smith, Sr. 183
Rickenbacker, Eddie 10
Ries, Al 13, 19, 162
Ries, Laura 19
The Right Report xii
RINOs 67
Roberts, Kevin 41
Robertson, Pat 76–77
Robert Wood Johnson Foundation 184
Robinson, Ron 101
Rockefeller Foundation 184
Roe, Thomas A. 183
Romney, Mitt 73
Rubio, Marco 18, 203
Ruddy, Chris 167
Rumsfeld, Donald 104
Rusher, Bill 8–9
Russia 28, 158
Ryan, Paul 73

Salem Media Group 167
Sanders, Bernie 51
Sarah Scaife Foundation 183
Scaife, Sarah 183

Scalise, Steve 67, 73
Schlafly, Phyllis *xiv,* 35, 76, 186
school choice 30
Schuchman, Robert 10
Schumer, Chuck 24, 26, 67, 71, 204
Schwarzman, Stephen A. 183
Scott, McKenzie 52
Sears, Alan 77
Second Amendment 30, 44, 95, 149, 177
Second Amendment Foundation 177
Senate Leadership Fund 174
Service Employees International Union 179
the sexual revolution 79
Shakespeare, William 148
Shapiro, Ben 95, 166
Shields, Vi 146
SHOT Show 168
Sierra Club 179
Sierra Club Foundation 179
Sinclair 95
Singer, Paul E. 183
Sixty Thirty Fund 180
smartphones 31
Smith, Adam 11
Smith Richardson Family Foundation 183
Smoot, Dan 7
socialism 1–2, 24–26, 28, 31–32, 40, 44–45, 48, 51, 53, 57, 59, 64, 67, 69, 71, 73, 98, 121, 147, 150–51, 158, 203
Social Security 62
Soros, George 52, 78, 155, 184
Southern Alliance for Clean Energy 181
Southern Poverty Law Center 180
Soviet Union 154
Spiritual Civil War 1, 92, 121, 147, 149–51, 157–59, 161
Stand Together 1, 175
State Department 151
statehood (for D.C., Puerto Rico) 29, 93, 149
State Policy Network 168, 175
Steiger, Sam 103
Stephen A. Schwarzman Foundation 183
Steyer, Tom 52, 78
Stone, Bob 81
Stone, Roger *viii*
The Strategic Coach 139–40, 142, 193
Sturm, Bob 160
Sullivan, Dan 139–43, 193
Sun Oil Company 10
Supreme Court 29, 62, 93
Susan B. Anthony List 176–77
Susan Thompson Buffett Foundation 184
Symms, Steve 111

Taft, Robert A. 7, 35
taglines 20–23, 86
Task Force for Global Health 180
taxes 29, 36, 44, 48, 57, 62, 93, 133, 135–37, 205
Tea Party 63, 79, 115
Templeton, John 183
term limits 149
Texas Public Policy Foundation 175
The Conservative Caucus 76, 165
The Nation magazine *viii*
Thomas A. Roe Foundation 183
Thomas B. Fordham Institute 177
Thompson, Frank 111
Thune, John 67, 73
Thurmond, Strom 35
Tides Advocacy 180
Tides Center 179
Tides Foundation 179
Tides Network 181
TIME Magazine 60
Tips 34, 167
Tower, John 7, 11, 35
Townhall.org 167
Treasury Department 103
Trout, Jack 13, 162
Trump, Donald 4–5, 21, 41, 54, 64, 75, 87, 166, 203
Trust for Public Lands 179
Turner, Daryl 27
Turning Point USA 168, 175
TVNewser 58
Twitter 27, 59, 63, 74, 94, 156

Uihlein, Ed 183
Ukraine 68
unemployment 27
unions 2, 4, 30, 38, 44, 52, 65, 67, 107–8, 120, 151
United Airlines 17
United Nations (UN) 149, 158
University of Houston 11
Urgent Action Fund for Women's Human Rights 181
U.S. News and World Report *ix*, 112

vaccinations 31, 44
veterans 39
Vietnam 42
Viguerie Company *ix, xii*, 110
Von Kannon, John 77, 127–28
voter ID 28, 65
Voter Registration Project 180

Waasdorp, Erica 87, 162
Walker, Bob 33
Walker, Scott 101
Wall Street 2, 9, 24, 59, 96, 151, 156
Wall Street Journal 9, 59, 96, 156
Warwick, Mal 162
Washington Examiner 167
Washington Free-Beacon 168
Washington Post *x*, 52, 60, 96, 108
Washington Star *x*, 34, 111
Washington Times *vii, ix*, 156, 168
Watergate 62
Watters, Jesse 14, 56, 64, 95, 166
Weber, Vin 33
welfare 27, 39, 46, 92, 129, 136
Weller, Charles E. 157
Western Center on Law & Poverty 181
Western Civilization *v*, 73, 122, 144, 149–50, 158, 161, 169, 192
Western CPAC 169
Western Journalism Center 56
Western Journal 168
Western Resource Advocates 181
Weyrich, Paul 33, 35–36, 110, 187
Whitewater scandal 114
Wilks, Dan & Staci 183
William and Flora Hewlett Foundation 184
William H. Donner Foundation 183
William Penn Foundation 184
Windward Fund 180
WinRed 174, 177
"woke" 31–32, 41, 151
World War II 158
World Wildlife Fund 179
Wren, Carter 105

X Prize Foundation 142

Yale University 9, 11
Yass, Jeffery 183
Young Americans for Freedom (YAF) 8–11, 75–76, 100–101, 103, 145, 165, 169
Young America's Foundation 165, 175
Youngkin, Glenn 22, 80, 203
Young Republicans *xii*, 7
YouTube 25, 59, 63, 74, 92, 156

Zuckerberg, Mark 52, 78, 155

Survey for *GO BIG* Readers

The results of this survey will be updated periodically and sent to political leaders, activists, and the national media. To take the survey online and/or check the results, go to ConservativeHQ.com or GoBigConservatives.com.

If you don't want to do the survey online, you can cut out these last four pages (two leaves), or photocopy them, to mail in.

1. I am a ☐ conservative ☐ libertarian ☐ moderate
    ☐ liberal ☐ socialist ☐ other

2. I usually vote ☐ Republican ☐ Democrat ☐ other

3. Rank your favorites for the 2024 Republican presidential nominee. Write #1 for your favorite, 2 for your second choice, and 3 for your third choice.

    ___ Greg Abbott
    ___ Tom Cotton
    ___ Ted Cruz
    ___ Ron DeSantis
    ___ Nikki Haley
    ___ Asa Hutchinson
    ___ Kristi Noem
    ___ Mike Pence
    ___ Mike Pompeo
    ___ Marco Rubio
    ___ Rick Scott
    ___ Tim Scott
    ___ Donald Trump
    ___ Glenn Youngkin
    ___ Other (write in) _____

4. Which of the following two statements best represents your feeling about the Republican leader in the U.S. House of Representatives, Kevin McCarthy?
    ☐ I like his policies and think he's a strong leader
    ☐ I think he compromises too much with Nancy Pelosi and other Democrats and I don't think he provides strong leadership for conservatives.

Continued on reverse . . .

5. Which of the following two statements best represents your feeling about the Republican leader in the U.S. Senate, Mitch McConnell?
☐ I like his policies and think he's a strong leader
☐ I think he compromises too much with Chuck Schumer and other Democrats and I don't think he provides strong leadership for conservatives.

6. What are your thoughts about Republican politicians? Check which statement best represents your thoughts.
☐ I'm a proud Republican and feel that most Republican politicians are providing good and strong leadership.
☐ I believe most Republican politicians are weak and don't provide strong, effective opposition to the Democrats.

To take the survey online and/or check the results go to ConservativeHQ.com or GoBigConservatives.com.

You can cut out or photocopy these page(s) and mail to:

Richard Viguerie
P.O. Box 1412
Manassas, VA 20108

Conservatives: How to Win Big
in the 2022 and 2024 Elections

Liberals have 2,000% more grassroots organizations and 700% more grassroots activists, which gives them a huge advantage at election time.

My goal is to raise $400,000 to send copies of *GO BIG* to 20,000 local conservative leaders to educate and encourage them to launch 20,000 new conservative organizations, which will encourage millions of conservatives to become modern-day Paul Reveres to educate 100,000,000 family, friends, and others to help us win big in the 2022 and 2024 elections.

Will you help?

☐ **$20** will allow us to send a copy of *GO BIG* to a local conservative leader and help grow the conservative movement 1,000%
☐ **$40** will allow us to send copies of *GO BIG* to 2 local conservative leaders and help grow the conservative movement 1,000%
☐ **$100** will allow us to send copies of *GO BIG* to 5 local conservative leaders and help grow the conservative movement 1,000%
☐ **$240** will allow us to send copies of *GO BIG* to 12 local conservative leaders and help grow the conservative movement 1,000%
☐ **$500** will allow us to send copies of *GO BIG* to 25 local conservative leaders and help grow the conservative movement 1,000%
☐ **$1,000** will allow us to send copies of *GO BIG* to 50 local conservative leaders and help grow the conservative movement 1,000%
☐ **$**_____ My Best Gift to get copies of *GO BIG* to local conservative leaders and help grow the conservative movement 1,000%

You can cut out or photocopy these page(s) and mail to:
Richard A. Viguerie
Go Big
P.O. Box 1412
Manassas, VA 20108

Give Copies of *GO BIG* to Family and Friends to Help
Grow the Conservative Movement 1,000%

If necessary, send a separate sheet of paper to include more names and addresses. Taxes, shipping, and handling are all included in the $20 price. Contributions are not tax deductible.

You can also contribute or order copies of GO BIG online at www.GoBigConservatives.com.

Continued on reverse . . .

Please send a copy of *GO BIG* to the following people:

_____

Name

_____

_____

Address

_____

City, State, Zip

_____

Name

_____

_____

Address

_____

City, State, Zip

_____

Name

_____

_____

Address

_____

City, State, Zip

_____

Name

_____

_____

Address

_____

City, State, Zip

**Amount enclosed for book purchases
($20 each)**

_____

**Amount I'm donating to give books to
local conservative leaders ($20 each)**

_____

Total enclosed

_____